REKINDLING THE PASSION

Liturgical Renewal in Your Community

Susan S. Jorgensen

Resource Publications, Inc.
San Jose, California

Editorial director: Kenneth Guentert
Managing editor: Elizabeth J. Asborno
Cover design: Br. Aelred-Seton Shanley
Cover production: Terri Ysseldyke-All

Reprint Department
Resource Publications, Inc.
160 E. Virginia Street #290
San Jose, CA 95112-5876

Library of Congress Cataloging in Publication Data
Jorgensen, Susan S., 1951-
    Rekindling the passion : liturgical renewal in your
community / Susan S. Jorgensen.
        p.   cm.
    Includes bibliographical references and index.
    ISBN 0-89390-236-5
    1. Catholic Church—Liturgy. 2. Church renewal—Catholic
Church. 3. Catholic Church—Membership. I. Title.
    BX1970.J62   1992
    264'.02'001—dc20   92-32396

97 96 95 94 93 | 5 4 3 2 1

for my family—
Jorg,
Amy, Matthew and Stacy
who are a sacrament of God's presence
in my daily life

and

for all whose love of liturgy
draws them into the heart of Christ
and *sets them on fire*

yes

GOD so

loved

the

WORLD that he
gave

his
only SON
that

WHOEVER

believes in him may
not die but may have

ETERNAL

life

✤ John 3:16

CONTENTS

PART I

THE WHOLE

PART III

TOWARD GREATER WHOLENESS

ACKNOWLEDGMENTS

Permission to quote excerpts from the following sources is gratefully acknowledged:

Scripture quotations are taken from the **New American Bible** Copyright © 1970 by the Confraternity of Christian Doctrine, Washington, D.C., and are used with permission. All rights reserved.

The Power of Myth, by Joseph Campbell with Bill Moyers, © 1988 Doubleday.

From The Liturgical Press: *The New Dictionary of Sacramental Worship*, copyright © 1991 by The Order of St. Benedict, Inc., published by The Liturgical Press, Collegeville, Minnesota, used with permission; *On Liturgical Theology*, copyright © 1984 by The Order of St. Benedict, Inc., published by The Liturgical Press, Collegeville, Minnesota, used with permission.

Reprinted from *Faith Development and Pastoral Care* by James Fowler, copyright © 1987 Fortress Press. Used by permission of Augsburg Fortress.

From The Pastoral Press: *Exploring the Sacred* by James Empereur, © 1987 The Pastoral Press; *Worship: Renewal to Practice* by Mary Collins, © 1987 The Pastoral Press; *Praying the Sacraments* by Peter Fink, © 1991 The Pastoral Press; *Liturgical Participation* by Frederick McManus, © 1988 The Pastoral Press.

The Evolving Self—Problem and Process in Human Development by Robert Kegan, © 1982 Harvard University Press.

From Paulist Press: *Inviting the Mystic, Supporting the Prophet: An Introduction to Spiritual Direction* by L. Patrick Carroll and Katherine Dyckman, © 1981 Paulist Press; *Spirituality and Personal Maturity* by Joann Wolski Conn, © 1989 Paulist Press; *Christian Conversion: A Developmental Interpretation of Autonomy and Surrender* by Walter Conn, © 1986 Paulist Press; *Liturgy, Prayer and Spirituality* by Kevin Irwin, © 1984 Paulist Press; *Carl Jung and Christian Spirituality* edited by Robert L. Moore, © 1988 Paulist Press.

Dry Bones by Robert Hovda, copyright The Liturgical Conference, 8750 Georgia Avenue, Suite 123, Silver Spring, Maryland, 20910-3621. All rights reserved. Used with permission.

"What to do if church is an 'occasion of sin'?" in *National Catholic Reporter* 28, no. 34 (July 17, 1992): 22. Reprinted with permission of National Catholic Reporter, P.O. Box 419281, Kansas City, Missouri, 64141.

For the Life of the World by Alexander Schmemann, © 1973 St. Vladimir's Seminary Press.

From HarperCollins Publishers Inc.: Excerpts from *The Magic of Ritual* by Tom Driver, Copyright © 1991 by Tom F. Driver, Reprinted by permission of HarperCollins Publishers; Excerpts from *Stages of Faith* by James Fowler, Copyright © 1981 by James Fowler, Reprinted by permission of HarperCollins Publishers; Excerpts from *Real Presence* by Regis Duffy, Copyright © 1982 by Harper & Row, Publishers, Inc., Reprinted by permission of HarperCollins Publishers; Excerpts from *Let This Mind Be in You* by Sebastion Moore, Copyright © 1985 by Sebastian Moore, Reprinted by permission of HarperCollins Publishers.

Quotations from the Vatican II Documents were taken from *Liturgy Documents: A Parish Resource* (Chicago: Liturgy Training Publications, 1985, Mary Ann Simcoe, editor) and are used by permission from the following copyright holders:

From the International Commission on English in the Liturgy: Excerpts from the English translation of the Constitution on the Liturgy and the General Instruction of the Roman Missal, fourth edition from *Documents on the Liturgy, 1963-1979: Conciliar*

Papal, and Curial Texts © 1982, International Committee on English in the Liturgy, Inc. (ICEL); excerpts from the English translation of the Introduction to the Lectionary for Mass, 2nd edition from *Lectionary for Mass* © 1981, ICEL. All rights reserved.

Excerpts are taken from the *Environemnt and Art in Catholic Worship* Copyright © 1978 by the United State Catholic Conference, Washington, D.C. and are used with permission. All rights reserved.

The following abbreviations were used for the documents quoted in this book:

◊ CSL — Constitution on the Sacred Liturgy

◊ GI — General Instruction on the Roman Missal

◊ LI — Lectionary for the Mass: Introduction

◊ EACW — Environment and Art in Catholic Worship

My heartfelt thanks go to many. First and foremost to Tom Musbach, without whom this book never would have come to fruition; to my gifted, patient, dedicated editor, Liz Asborno, whose thoughts and comments have brought greater clarity and organization to nearly every page; to Joseph Marcucio, Mary Blume, Carol Storey, Ken Suibielski, and Bob Burbank, who read every word and gave me many good insights; to Jim Keegan, who read portions of the manuscript and inspired me to write about personal ritual; to Aelred-Seton Shanley, who gave me a quiet, gentle space in which to begin this project; to Andrée Grafstein, who worked many long hours with me in organizing and presenting the eight-week program on liturgical renewal in parishes; to Ann Marie Caron, whose course on worship was the primary inspiration for this work; to my spiritual directors—Mark, Liz, Joe and Tony—who have all helped me to see God's amazing revelations in my life and work—I bring those revelations to each page of this book; to all the wonderful women in my internship program in spiritual direction—Moira, Mary, Ginger, Linda, Ellen, Donna, Yvonne, Mary, Elizabeth and Maureen—their journeys and wisdom have graced my life in untold ways; and, finally, to my family, whose constant love and support kept me going through this very amazing process.

PREFACE

When we speak of liturgy...we are speaking of the
deed so utterly central to the Christian life that all
depends on it...and without it there is no covenant
people and no church. — Robert Hovda[1]

Genesis. In the beginning. The story of how this book
came to the attention of its publisher is a remarkable one,
one that is too long for telling here. With the plethora of
material on liturgy and renewal that is currently available,
I hesitate to contribute another piece and yet, my perspective and purpose, while not unique, are different. I write
not as a theologian or a liturgist. I write as a spiritual director
whose focus, love and training has been and continues to
be about relationship with God. I am convinced that this
relationship is carried out in both the personal and communal realms. It is through both personal prayer and communal worship that God seeks to touch God's people. One
nourishes and works in tandem with the other and both
must be tended and cared for, cherished and treasured. "Of
its very nature, liturgical prayer must lead to private prayer;

---

[1] Hovda, *Dry Bones,* 48.

private prayer, in its turn, prepares the way for even deeper liturgical worship."[2] And so to look not only at the dynamics of personal prayer and relationship with God, as spiritual directors do, but to look at the dynamics of the communal as well seems to be a natural outgrowth of my work and training.

This book began as a thesis for my master's degree in pastoral ministry; its roots lie in an eight-week program that I developed with a friend. The primary focus of the program was to encourage people to *pray* the liturgy, more specifically eucharistic liturgy. We presented this program twice—once on the parish level and once at our own Archdiocesan Spiritual Life Center. The components of the program included communal prayer, personal reflection, group sharing and catechesis. Working with these people was a great gift, profound and grace-filled. Their presence is manifest on each and every page of this book, and I owe my heartfelt gratitude to all of them; their response to the program has supported and encouraged me throughout this effort.

My thesis sought to articulate all upon which we had drawn in the process of developing and implementing the program. This book, as an outgrowth of that goal, is guided by this and is shaped very specifically by three questions. The first is, "What do we need to know in order to help us to pray liturgy better?" The answer is at once simple and complex. Simplicity is secure within the heart of God; complexity within the heart of this decade of the twentieth century. It would be foolish for us not to be informed to the best of our abilities in this technological age; foolish also not to protect and hold dear the simplicity. The tension is obvious; the balance, a delicate one.

As Christians, we find ourselves at a fortuitous time in our history. We have worlds of knowledge that is applicable and enlightening to any examination of liturgy. This knowl-

---

2 Egan, *Christian Mysticism*, 219. Egan here is discussing Thomas Merton's perspective about daily Mass.

edge is more readily available than at any other point in our history. No longer is it appropriate or timely to limit our study to theology. We need to draw on the vast body of knowledge made available through psychology, sociology, and most recently, the rich field of anthropology. It is from these vast, varied, and yet complementary, fields that we attempt to answer the question of "what."

The second question, "How will all of this help us to pray our liturgies better?" is a theoretical one. It is hoped that, by asking some specific questions from time to time based on the material being presented, avenues for action might open up for the reader. Keep in mind that every community has its own needs, resources and limitations and that you are the best judge of your community's.

The third question is, "For whom is this book intended?" The "we" of the question, "What do we need to know?" encompasses all of our parish leaders, our liturgical ministers, our pastoral associates—the people "in the trenches," so to speak. But it does not stop there. The "we" is also every person who enters into the liturgical celebration. As we become more involved and open during liturgy, the encompassing mystery of God will touch us and move us to touch those around us. Called by God, we all have a shared responsibility to answer God's invitation to become instruments of God's love and revelation.

So much hard, earnest, brilliant work has been done in the field of liturgy and renewal—one needs only look at the countless titles on the book shelves or in a card catalog. What remains a mystery, at least to me, is why the impact of this work on the actual liturgies in our communities seems to be minimal.[3] Our worship often remains a chore, a task on our ever-lengthening list of things to do. Most of us have attended liturgies that are truly moving, that truly embody and realize the prophetic vision of Vatican II. Some

---

[3] Aidan Kavanagh offers some interesting reflections regarding the gulf between the pastoral and the academic in his book, *On Liturgical Theology,* 17-19.

of us are fortunate to have this be the rule rather than the exception. For many of us, however, this type of liturgical experience remains the exception. The logical question then, for me, becomes "Why?" especially considering the wealth of material that is available.

From this pondering emerges a tentative theory that the bulk of this material is not reaching those who really need and hunger for it: those of us who labor in the fields, who struggle with the complexity of our lives, who delicately (and sometimes not so delicately) juggle a myriad of daily tasks and commute in rush-hour traffic. The resources available are not reaching the ordinary people who faithfully serve in parishes, on their councils and various committees *and* the people who pastor them.

This book attempts to remedy this situation by bridging the gap between the academic and the pastoral. It attempts to translate into a simpler language the often complex sentence structures and word choices found in academic treatises. At the same time, it attempts to remain faithful to the content of the academic work. It draws upon many academic disciplines and attempts to weave them into a coherent whole. This is not an easy task, and I ask the reader's patience, understanding and forgiveness when the result falls short of the goal.

Regarding inclusive language for references to God, I have stayed away from substituting any pronoun for "God" (except in certain Scripture passages) because God is everything in all of us. It is no more correct to refer to God as "she" as it is to refer to God as "he." Therefore some sentences may sound awkward (I can see my high school English teacher poised with red pen, ready to edit all such sentences!), but they are accurate. After all, we should not attempt to compromise God in service of the English language; in this case, the English language asks to be compromised in service of God.

It is an honor and a privilege to be with you through the pages of this book. In my writing and your reading, our journeys intersect and become one for a time. It is my heartfelt hope that this writing and reading be a modest portion of

> the work of the kindness of our God;
> he, the Dayspring, shall visit us in his mercy
> to shine on those who sit in darkness
> and in the shadow of death,
> to guide our feet into the way of peace
> (Luke 1:78-79).

Hermitage of the Dayspring
11 January 1992

INTRODUCTION

The renewal in the eucharist of the covenant
between the Lord and his people
draws the faithful into the compelling love of Christ
and *sets them on fire.*
— Constitution on the Sacred Liturgy[1]

Liturgy is about loving and being loved. God reveals
Godself in this process. Learning to love and be loved will
change us in ways that are not comfortable or easy—they
will set us on fire. I would like to share with you a passage
from the Velveteen Rabbit because it illustrates simply and
well what liturgy is about:

> "What is REAL?" asked the Rabbit one day. "Does
> it mean having things that buzz inside you and a
> stick-out handle?"
> "Real isn't how you are made," said the Skin
> Horse. "It's a thing that happens to you. When a
> child loves you for a long, long time, not just to play
> with, but REALLY loves you, then you become Real."
> "Does it hurt?"

---

[1] CSL, n. 10; my emphasis.

"Sometimes." For he was always truthful. "When you are Real you don't mind being hurt."

"Does it happen all at once, like being wound up, or bit by bit?"

"It doesn't happen all at once. You become. It takes a long time. That's why it doesn't often happen to people who break easily, or who have sharp edges, or who have to be carefully kept. Generally, by the time you are Real, most of your hair has been loved off, and your eyes drop out and you get loose in the joints and very shabby.

"But these things don't matter at all, because once you are Real you can't be ugly, except to people who don't understand."

The Rabbit sighed. He thought it would be a long time before this magic called Real happened to him. He longed to become Real, to know what it felt like; and yet the idea of growing shabby and losing his eyes and whiskers was rather sad. He wished that he could become it without these uncomfortable things happening to him..."[2]

Much has, can and will be said about liturgy; this book is but one example of how much can be said about liturgy. But I believe any discussion about liturgy should begin and end with the experience of love described so well in this simple children's story. This love is compelling, and it brings about change that does not always initially feel good. Liturgy is a process of paradox—we long to be a part of the becoming and yet we also fear it. If we understand that liturgy in its most profound experience is about love and conversion and our paradoxical "both/and" response to this process, then much of what is said here about liturgy will be more completely understood.

Adulthood often makes complexity look attractive. It is good to start with this simple children's story; Jesus tells us that "what you have hidden from the learned and the clever you have revealed to the merest children" (Mt 11:25).

---

[2] Williams, *Velveteen Rabbit.*

Again, I do believe that much of what is said in this excerpt reveals the dynamic that is operative in our liturgical celebrations: we long to enter the process completely and we fear that it will not always feel good. My own sense is that renewal must be rooted in an acute awareness of this dynamic. We need to look at how to encourage the desire ("he longed to become Real") and how to embrace and work through our very human fears ("he wished that he could become it without these uncomfortable things happening to him").

And no, the passage does not touch upon ritual studies, theological treatises or developmental theory. It does not touch upon the meaning and use of symbolism in our liturgical celebrations, participation or what it means to be "Church." But there is an essential understanding in this excerpt from *The Velveteen Rabbit* that is crucial to all that follows. We need to read this passage over and over again until we fully comprehend what it means to be so loved ("for God so loved the world that he gave his only Son"), what it means to be changed by this love ("that whoever believes in him may not die but may have eternal life" [Jn 3:16]), and how we feel about the process of love and change (we long for it *and* we wish it didn't have to happen). Our renewal efforts will find a heart within the context of love. These efforts will find a home through the understanding that conflicting feelings are a natural part of the conversion process.

My initial captivation with liturgy began several years ago. At that time, I was struck by the delicate movement that all liturgy seems to have, and I was deeply moved by it. Through its subtle motion, liturgy reconciles seemingly opposite experiences—light and dark, life and death, pain and joy, giving and receiving. Through its rhythm, liturgy expresses its magic and its mystery. Through its dance, it reveals the profound presence of God without overwhelming those who experience it. Through my gradual awareness of this process of motion, rhythm and dance, I came to know something of the breath-taking beauty of liturgy.

And then, in 1988, I had the privilege of attending the Religious Educators' East Coast Conference in Washington, D.C. The liturgical celebration was very moving—amidst some 1,500 people, we could feel the Spirit among us; every word and gesture, prayer and action was incredibly alive. Most of us could say that it was an experience of incarnational liturgy, of Christ truly present in and through everyone and everything. Very few remained untouched. And yet, there we were, strangers gathered together for one moment in time. There we were in the middle of a large conference room. Great attention had been given to the environment, but it remained nonetheless a conference room. It is true that many of the liturgical ministers were very well trained at what they did; some were even nationally known. Planning for the liturgy had been carried out carefully; no detail had been overlooked. It is also true that energy levels were high and that all of us present had gathered with a great desire to worship together. And worship we did! Frederick McManus' statement that "the liturgy is the work of Christ, in the Spirit, more than it is our work,"[3] was never more true than it was that day. I have also experienced liturgies like that one during other conferences and in private homes; to a lesser degree during parish weekday celebrations and at retreat houses; and, sadly, much less frequently during parish Sunday liturgies.

These experiences have led me in search of "why." Why some liturgies and not others? Why some assemblies and not others? What makes liturgies "work?" "Work" here is not meant to indicate the experience of "good feelings and peak experiences"; liturgy is not about feeling good. "Work" here is meant to indicate the experience of the radical "presence of God calling us to presence."[4] Liturgy

---

[3] McManus, *Liturgical Participation*, 33.

[4] Duffy, *Real Presence*, 3.

"works" when the assembly deeply experiences Christ as "always present in his Church...present in the sacrifice of the Mass...present in the sacraments...present in his word...present when the Church prays and sings" (CSL, n. 7). Liturgy "works" when it is experienced as prayer, covenantal relationship, commitment to gospel values and mission. Several years ago, a friend remarked that, if we truly experienced the power of Eucharist, the walls of the church building itself would explode with the energy. Hyperbole? Perhaps, but something in her statement has the ring of truth in it.

And so, we are faced with a sea of questions when we address what makes liturgy "work." Is it the depth of commitment in the particular assembly? Is it the level and degree of planning? Is it the skill of the liturgical ministers? Is there some formula that will insure the "full and active participation by all the people" (CSL, n. 14) more completely? What can be done to help us experience liturgy in all its fullness more of the time? In other words, what can be done to help us to pray together as one voice, one body in and through the presence of Christ?

These questions are about renewal. It has long been recognized that the initial reform and the catechesis that accompanied it were only the beginning. If, at one time, in our naiveté, we thought that once all the changes were technically implemented, the task would be complete and the vision of Vatican II realized, there are few who adhere to that view today.

Liturgical renewal requires intensive effort, especially if it is to become more than a polite discussion of the topic, if it is to move from the theoretical to the practical, from something that we might do "some day" to something that is a vital force in our communities. Part of this effort must be outer-directed, toward exploring the many facets of liturgy. We must look at what we do, who we are as we do it, what liturgy asks of us, and what tools we use. Part of this effort must be inner-directed, toward reflecting upon the holy other who is revealed during liturgy. We must learn to "be" in God's presence, to notice God, to allow God to reach out and touch us. This happens in the most interior part of our personal and communal bodies.

These are key issues that have at their root a need for education that is process- rather than end-oriented, a need for a deeper awareness of our actions and a need for honest reflection on the meaning of those actions. This education, awareness and reflection must happen on both personal and communal levels. I firmly believe that you have the talent needed for transforming renewal right in your own community. This book is meant to be a small spark and simple guide for that talent.

A Brief Overview

Part I of this work will look at liturgy as a whole. The word "liturgy" comes from the Greek words, *leitos,* which means "public," and *érgon*, which means "work": public work. It has come to mean all prescribed forms (rites and rituals) that are used for public worship. A deeper theological understanding of the word is reflected in the definition of liturgy as those "ritual words and gestures that are planned and yet not merely planned...which protect man from the direct experience of the sacred, but also keep him in touch with it—which is necessary since it is the source of life."[5] Our focus here is specifically eucharistic liturgy, more commonly referred to as "the Mass." And while this is true, many of the points made here can be applied to other forms of public worship and sacrament; there is no clear-cut delineation and no need to be exclusive. For the sake of brevity, the word "liturgy" only will be used in this book, keeping in mind, however, its focus on eucharistic liturgy in particular.

---

[5] Haughton, *Transformation of Man,* 79-80.

In looking at the whole, we will look broadly at the liturgical reform called for by Vatican II—what were its hopes and it goals and how well have they been realized? What remains to be done?

In turning toward the liturgy itself, we will look at our worship first through the lens of ritual. This is a relatively new lens for liturgical studies and one that has already yielded and promises to continue yielding a significant understanding of the many layers of activity that occur during liturgy. We will also develop a metaphor based on the process of weaving in order to describe the various things that we "do" during our liturgies.

We will ask the question, "What does it mean to be assembly?" We come from many different places and many different walks of life. And yet, in the act of assembling for liturgy, we are formed into a whole. I choose this phrase carefully—"we are formed" vs. "we become"—because it speaks more clearly of the divine initiative at work in our lives. This "whole" is community; it is Church; is is assembly; it is Body of Christ.

To understand who we are and what God calls us to do is not enough. We must begin to look at how we are asked to worship. The Vatican II documents state this clearly in the often-quoted text, "full and active participation by all the people is the aim to be considered before all else." The Constitution goes on to tell us why. This active participation is seen as "*the primary and indispensable source* from which the faithful are to derive the *true Christian spirit*" (CSL, n. 14; my emphasis). And while this is stated simply, the question of active participation is a complex one, involving all aspects of the human person: mind, body and soul.

Part II of this book will look at the particular pieces that make up the whole. If we look at our own eucharistic liturgy, we see that the pieces that comprise the whole, as well as the whole itself, are symbolic in nature. When some one/thing/action becomes symbolic in nature, it becomes "more than" ordinary; it has an energy that will draw its participants into a broader, deeper level of experience and meaning.

When we are able to honestly relate to our symbols, active participation begins to happen. Active participation is our conscious assent to the revelation inherent in all symbols; we say "yes" to our symbols, and they draw us into their mysterious process. Participation becomes an open exchange between the unseen mysteries of God and the depth of our being that unfolds in both head and heart, individually and communally. I see this as crucial to our efforts toward a vital, ongoing renewal.

Once we have looked at symbols, we will look at the individual members who comprise the liturgical assembly. Because liturgy reveals and expresses relationship—God with God's people, the people with their God—understanding how we relate to God and how God relates to us will be helpful. At the moment that we begin to address relationship, we enter into the realm of development. For two average toddlers, relationship is side-by-side play. For two fully mature adults, relationship is intentional, selfless giving to the other that simply seeks to be expressed in freedom, respect and reverence as an end unto itself. Between these two levels of relationship, there is an enormous span of themes and variations.

> We live in a process of growth; a development in
> which there are identifiable stages. Corresponding
> to our psychological stage of development is our
> experience of God and also our prayer.[6]

How our individual process of development affects our communal experience of God and prayer is an important issue for liturgical renewal. How this process influences our ability to participate during the various parts of the liturgy is also an important issue. These issues can be

---

[6] Manly and Reinhard, *Art of Praying Liturgy*, 117.

addressed in part through an exploration of developmental theory.

There is an additional benefit to exploring developmental theory, one that may not be obvious at first glance. This benefit is the growth of a deeper appreciation of and reverence toward one another. What holds true for one person does not necessarily hold true for another. The differences between us are not only the obvious physical ones. Some are created by the various roles that we adopt; some arise out of where we are psychologically and spiritually. Developmental theory articulates these differences. Opening up avenues to conduct dialogue about our psychological and spiritual growth can build bridges between us as we are called together to be the intimate and mystical Body of Christ. Earnest dialogue gives birth to an increased sensitivity to and respect for our individual uniqueness. This will help us to see our many differences as gifts rather than obstacles, as variations in the way God's presence is revealed in community.

In his first letter to the Corinthians, St. Paul praises our differences as essential to the functioning of the one body. I believe that a modern understanding of these differences (an understanding based upon developmental theory) will lead us to a greater peace with each other where "there may be no dissension in the body, but that all the members may be concerned for one another" (1 Cor 12:25). Full, active participation depends on our willingness to become Body of Christ; this willingness depends, in part, on our acceptance and appreciation of one another's differences: physical, social, psychological and spiritual. Developmental theory encourages this acceptance and appreciation.

The final chapter in Part II will look at culture. Communities, the individuals that comprise them, and the symbols that they use during worship do not exist in a vacuum. They are tied to a specific time and place, i.e., to a culture. This culture will exert a certain influence on all of these elements and vice versa. What are our dominant cultural values, goals, messages and hopes? How do they affect our

ability to enter into communal prayer, our ability to cooperate with divine grace and revelation? To look at these
dynamics is to set renewal into a context and to reveal some
of the important, underlying tensions that are created by
our very act of worship.

Part III applies many of the principles that form the
substance of this book. It offers some general suggestions
and some concrete ideas and programs to further liturgical
renewal in your community. It also presents a theory of
pastoral care that I believe is essential to successful renewal
efforts. We must first recognize that, on a very basic level,
renewal efforts are efforts toward caring for one another.
The underlying essence/presence that shapes all pastoral
care is the essence/presence of God. As pastoral care givers, we express God's essence/presence in seven different
ways:

◊ in community

◊ in mutuality

◊ in inclusiveness

◊ in vision

◊ in orientation toward growth

◊ in support and confrontation

◊ in reflection on experience

Most of us do not think of liturgy and liturgical renewal
in terms of pastoral care. But I believe that it is essential to
begin to do so. When we apply this definition of pastoral
care to liturgy, we put on the mind of Christ, we embrace
his vision, and we spread his gift out into the daily world.
To be celebrants of liturgy in every sense of the word is to
be pastoral care givers to all who come into our lives.

Liturgy asks that we see God in the communities we form
when we gather for worship. Liturgy asks that we exercise

mutuality and inclusiveness toward all who come to table. Liturgy asks that we have a vision of what is and is to come—Christ in our midst. Liturgy is a profound orientation toward growth. Liturgy supports and challenges us. Liturgy is a reflection of our deepest experiences of Christ among us. Liturgy is the essence and presence of God. Liturgy is the deepest embodiment of pastoral care.

Many topics are covered here. Due to the breadth of the work, it does not pretend to provide depth in any area. I hope that enough will be said about each topic that you will be able to apply it to your work in renewal; that you will recognize some connections between all the topics; and that you will strive to nurture those connections.

I hope that what is said will open your eyes, ears, minds and hearts to more concrete ways of helping your liturgical celebrations fully resonate and reside in the depth of your very being. I hope that renewal becomes the rekindling of passion—Christ's passion for us and our passion for Christ— as we are called by God to celebrate it during each and every liturgy.

PART I

THE WHOLE

CHAPTER 1

How Far Have We Come?

That something is wrong with the sacramental life
of most churches is a thought so widespread it
scarcely needs arguing. — Tom Driver[1]

The Vision of Vatican Council II

Vatican II set into motion changes in the Church as had
not been experienced since the late Middle Ages. We must
not underestimate the far-reaching effects of the Council,
not only in the Church but also in the world. We must not
underestimate the thought and care that went into the call
for change. Those who participated in the Council were
guided throughout by a dynamic vision, a vision that became the first paragraph of the first document published
by the Council. It is appropriate to state its guiding vision
at the outset of this chapter:

> This Sacred Council has several aims in view: it
> desires to *impart an ever increasing vigor* to the

---

[1] Driver, *Magic of Ritual*, 195.

Christian life of the faithful; to *adapt more suitably*
to the needs of our own times...to foster whatever
can *promote union among all* who believe in
Christ; to *strengthen whatever can help* to call the
whole of humanity into the household of the
Church (CSL, n. 1; my emphasis).

This vision is broad and inspirational. It is life-giving
("imparts an ever-increasing vigor"); it is sensitive to
change ("adapts more suitably to the needs of our own
times"); it desires a deeper sense of wholeness ("promotes
union among all who believe in Christ"); it embraces an
openness that is enviable ("strengthens whatever can
help"). It is important to come back to this vision again and
again; it forms the cornerstone of the entire Vatican II
renewal.

The vision is not rigid, iconoclastic, closed or reactionary.
It is *broad* in its method to impart increasing vigor; it is
prophetic in its realization that adaptation is needed; it is
inclusive in its aim to promote union; it is *daring* in its
willingness to strengthen whatever can help to call the
whole of humanity. To embrace this vision is to embrace
God's vision. This vision embodies a desire, hope and
dream that are God's desire, hope and dream as interpreted
through the voices of the many hundreds of God's people.

This excerpt from the Constitution on the Sacred Liturgy
provides us with some excellent guidelines. We need to ask
ourselves questions about the progress of liturgical renewal
based on the aims articulated in the CSL's first paragraph:

◊ How have our efforts toward renewal
   imparted an ever-increasing vigor to the
   Christian life? How have they hindered its
   development? Key to this set of questions is
   the development of a method to assess
   increasing vigor.

◊ How have our efforts adapted to the needs
   of our own times? How have our efforts

conflicted with them (keeping in mind that conflict does not necessarily indicate failure but the presence of a healthy challenge to those needs)? Key to this set of questions is an understanding of those needs.

◊ How have our efforts promoted union with Christ and among all whose faith is anchored in him? How have they created dissension? Key to this set of questions is an understanding of union—what does union look like and how does it feel when it happens?

◊ How have our efforts begun to call the whole of humanity into the household of the Church? How have they created alienation?

These questions are not easy ones; neither are they meant to be rhetorical. They have no quick answers, but they are key to assessing how well the vision of Vatican II has been realized. It is not an accident that this is the first paragraph of the first document issued by the Council; it establishes a tone and lays the foundation for all that was and is to follow. These questions have no specific audience; by that, I mean that it is important that they be addressed to and answered by the global Church. It is equally important that they also be addressed to and answered by each individual diocese and parish.

Recommendations of the Council

Much of the Vatican II vision expressed in this first paragraph of the Constitution on the Sacred Liturgy translated into a drive to achieve fuller participation in liturgy. This was done with a desire to be "open to legitimate progress" (CSL, n. 23) and with a caution that whatever was done should be rooted in our long Christian tradition.

The question of our Christian tradition raises some interesting questions regarding historical and liturgical scholarship.[2] And while we must be careful not to get sidetracked in our discussion here, it is important to note the great benefits of acquiring knowledge of our rich tradition. In learning about this tradition, we discover a sense of unity with all who have gone before us, a sense of Christian community that transcends time and place. In knowing how and why our liturgical practices originated and gradually evolved, we gain a greater understanding and appreciation of the rite as it is now.

The Church (particularly its pastors [see CSL, n. 14, paragraph 3]) was charged with achieving this fuller participation by placing a stronger emphasis on:

◊ Scripture (CSL, n. 24)

◊ communal involvement of the whole Body
of the Church (CSL, n. 26-30)

◊ catechesis (CSL, n. 35.3)

◊ conversion to the vernacular
(CSL, n. 36.2 & 3)

◊ the use of adaptation (CSL, n. 37)

What is surprising is that the change to vernacular was one of the most obvious to the average church-goer, but its implementation was not clearly mandated in the documents. The bishops were given the power to determine "whether and to what extent the vernacular [was] to be

---

2   Baldovin, *Worship: City, Church and Renewal.* On page 192, Fr.
    Baldovin makes an interesting case for scholarly research that is more
    critical than has been the case in the past. He cites several examples
    and cautions that we need to exercise more care in our efforts toward
    our determinations of what has been normative in our tradition.

used" (CSL, n. 36.3) and the Constitution took steps to encourage Latin as "the faithful" desired (CSL, n. 54).
We can commend the clear call for adaptation:

> ...the Church has no wish to impose a rigid
> uniformity in matters that do not affect the faith or
> the good of the whole community; rather, the
> Church respects and fosters the genius and talents
> of the various races and peoples. The Church
> considers with sympathy and, if possible, preserves
> intact the elements in these peoples' way of life that
> are not indissolubly bound up with superstition and
> error (CSL, n. 37).[3]

This picture of the Church as flexible and open is not one that many of us in the American culture have. Note 37 has an important message. Reflecting upon it, the words that clearly resonate are "respect," "genius," "talent," "sympathy" and "preservation." This note draws a picture of Church that is truly catholic—open to the whole world—and truly respectful of diversity. It also recognizes the need to foster and maintain the unity that is so important for us in our journey toward becoming universal Body of Christ.

Other specific recommendations in the Constitution include:

◊ promotion of the practice of receiving
  Communion under both species (CSL, n. 55;
  GI, n. 14 & 240; and GI app., n. 240 & 242)

◊ distribution of hosts consecrated only at the
  Mass being celebrated (GI, n. 56h)

◊ bread that is broken (GI, n. 56c)

---

[3] Although there is a qualifying phrase here, this passage expresses a healthy recognition of differences and a willingness to incorporate those differences where possible.

These recommendations stem from a recognition of and an appreciation for the deep symbolism of the Eucharist itself. Another significant change was the turning around of the altar so that the presider would face the assembly (GI, n. 262). In a separate section entitled "Promotion of Liturgical Instruction and Active Participation," the CSL made provisions for liturgical formation of the clergy (CSL, n. 14-18) and catechesis of the assembly (CSL, n. 19). The catechesis of the assembly was called "*one of the chief duties* [of the pastors] as faithful stewards of the mysteries of God" (CSL, n. 19; my emphasis). There are many more changes that flowed from the vision of the Council; these are the highlights that produced very obvious results.

The Task Ahead: New Directions

Much was accomplished in the first twenty-five years following the close of the Council; there can be no doubt about this. However, what remains to be done goes deeper; using our bodies in prayer, reclaiming mystery, restructuring Church, and modifying harmful attitudes are all at the heart of the second wave of renewal. These are not easy tasks, and they will require long-term commitment on our part.

Using Our Bodies in Prayer

A universal call to holiness and a desire to touch the *whole* of humanity were at the heart of the Vatican II changes. One way we could do this was to place greater importance on our bodies:

> We learn from the same Apostle [Paul] that we must always bear about in our body the dying of Jesus, so that the life also of Jesus may be made manifest *in our bodily frame*" (CSL, n. 12; my emphasis).

This is an explicit call to a holistic spirituality that embraces both body and spirit, the human and the divine; no longer do we need to be hampered by these artificial divisions. A "holistic spirituality which adheres to God at the center of everything and seeks to cooperate with God in bringing God's reign into every sphere of life"[4] has begun to evolve as a direct result of the Vatican II initiatives.

To understand how revolutionary this shift is, one must remember that the very definition of spirituality created a rigid, unbridgeable dichotomy between body and spirit for a long period of time in Church history. The living of the spiritual life called for the strict abandonment of the physical world, including the body. Bringing God's reign into every sphere of life breaks down the false separation between body, world and spirit. It restores God's reign to the place it honestly belongs—within the realm of our bodies and our everyday world. It opens the door for us to truly experience and celebrate one of the least-celebrated gifts of Jesus. By taking our human form, he gave honor to it in a way that nothing or no one else could.

For many centuries in our Christian tradition, we could not celebrate this gift because the human form was the very thing that we tried to ignore, purge and punish and from which we tried to separate ourselves.[5] Thankfully, many of us are not there anymore, but we have far to go in terms of being comfortable with our bodies. All we need to do is look at how impoverished most of our liturgical gestures are; this clearly indicates how far we have to go. Until we reach a deeper comfort level with our "physicalness," the bearing of the dying Jesus in our own bodies will not be fully realized; the manifestation of Christ in our bodies will

---

4   Joann Wolski Conn, *Spirituality and Personal Maturity,* 28.

5   Ernest Becker's book, *Denial of Death,* gives a very detailed perspective of this attitude from a psychological point of view. It is very enlightening for those who wish to gain a deeper understanding of this issue.

be recognized and expressed imperfectly, as an already but not yet.

Reclaiming the Experience of Mystery

The environmental changes mandated by Vatican II resulted in greater participation: we pray in our own native language and the priest faces the assembly.

> With the altar now facing the people, there is obviously more sense of communication on both sides, and much less danger of the old wool-gathering distractedness.[6]

We have more of a sense of what is going on throughout the liturgy and we are more involved in it. Yet, we have also lost something very precious. Joseph Campbell, in *The Power of Myth*, wisely and humorously observes:

> There's been a reduction of ritual. Even in the Roman Catholic Church, my God—they've translated the Mass out of ritual language and into a language that has a lot of domestic associations. The Latin of the Mass was a language that threw you *out* of the field of domesticity. The altar was turned so that the priest's back was to you, and with him you addressed yourself outward. Now they've turned the altar around—it looks like Julia Child giving a demonstration—all homey and cozy.[7]

This is not a statement of advocacy for the return of Latin or for a change in the position of the altar. But it does bring out the fact that there has been a loss, and that loss is primarily one of mystery.

There has been an exposure with the advent of the vernacular that has fed into our technological need to know

---

6 Merton, *Seasons of Celebration*, 232.

7 Campbell, *Power of Myth*, 84.

all there is to know about *everything*. Joseph Campbell's acute observation should give pause for thought. Johannes Emminghaus addresses the issue in a somewhat more theological way that is not quite so flippant: "We must not allow the removal of the language barriers to lead to a complete verbalization of the liturgy; the mystery must be respected."[8] In order to recapture our appreciation of mystery without returning to Latin, the symbolism of the liturgy must be renewed. The heart of symbolism is mystery: the living presence of a loving God, a risen Christ and a life lived in and through the Spirit. What has been lost in language can be recovered through greater engagement with the symbolic structure. What has been lost through our technological advances can be recovered through a greater acceptance and appreciation of mystery.

Restructuring Church

For all its vision, the Council retained its pre-Vatican II hierarchical structure. This structure has often found itself in opposition to the aims of the Council; hierarchy does not often work well within a body that aims to be more life–giving, sensitive to change, whole and open. As a result, friction and disillusionment have ensued. We have at least partially achieved many of the aims stated in the opening paragraph of the CSL:

◊ An increasing vigor has been set free; the non-ordained have taken active roles in leadership and ministry.

◊ Adaptation has become more widespread, encouraging greater participation (for example, more singing, frequent reception of Eucharist).

---

8 Emminghaus, *Eucharist*, xv.

◊ A sense of union among all who believe in
Christ has become deeper and more solid;
there is definitely a greater understanding of
and identification with the priesthood of all
believers.

These achievements have strained the existing structure
severely. It was Jesus himself who said that we could not
pour new wine into old wineskins.[9] The parable speaks
clearly to us in this last decade of the second millennium
as we watch our old wineskins sag and tear under the
pressures created by the new freedoms that have arisen
through the conciliar efforts. Until this is somehow re-
solved (and the issue grows more serious daily with an
increasing shortage of priests and a corresponding refusal
to alter the structure), the gap between the old and the new
will grow. The vision of the Council will continue to
produce a tension that, at this juncture in our journey, I
would call creative. If we continue to push the issue under
the rug, the tension may become destructive.

Modifying Our Attitudes

I believe that this issue is closely tied to both our lack of
engagement with our symbols and to the anachronisms of
the hierarchical structure mentioned above. Changes in
any of them will result in changes in all. Thomas Merton
addresses these attitudes succinctly in *Seasons of Celebration.*

The first of these attitudes is a consuming concern with
doctrine and correctness of ritual. This is the familiar battle
of the law versus the spirit, faith versus works—a common
theme in the letters of Paul. "No one is justified in God's
sight by the law, for 'the just man shall live by faith'" (Gal
3:11). Yet we continue to promote the law and we end up

---

[9] See Mark 3:22.

with empty, mechanical ritual. We continue to practice secondary theology that develops doctrine that does not respect or cooperate with the lived experience and the faith of the assembly. This is much easier and less threatening than speaking from a faith stance that continually calls us to conversion and deeper commitment. We need to counteract the false sense of security we get when we cling too tightly to doctrine and law that is removed from what is real in our lives. We need the courage, opportunity and nurturing environment in which to reflect upon our faith and our experience. Ritual comes alive when it mirrors that faith and experience.

The second attitude is one which affects our approach to and interaction with each other. All the renewal in the world will not bring about lasting change if it is not done with the right spirit, the "new spirit of openness, in which the priest is open to his people, and they are open to him and one another." [10] This openness must be informed by the sacramental presence of Christ in his Church: he is "always present in his Church, especially in its liturgical celebrations" (CSL, n. 7). It is Christ who must guide us by his moving example of inclusive, loving service and the reverence he exhibited toward those he served.

The Task Ahead: Specific Goals

We have not, for the most part, met some of the obvious, tangible goals set out by the Council. Again, this is said with some hesitation, as in some communities these goals have been met consistently and creatively. But for many of us, the goals are still goals, not a reality that we experience in our regular worship. There are many that could be highlighted; the ones presented here have been carefully cho-

---

[10] Merton, *Seasons of Celebration*, 236.

sen. I believe that the unmet goals cited here are symptomatic of deeper issues: our inability to relate well to our Christian symbols and the problems with the hierarchical structure.

The Communion Rite

How many of us experience Communion under both species? In 1985, the National Conference of Catholic Bishops issued a publication entitled, *This Holy and Living Sacrifice, Directory for the Celebration and Reception of Communion under Both Kinds*. In 1991, the Federation of Diocesan Liturgical Commissions (FDLC) published a two-page document by Andrew D. Ciferni, O.Praem., entitled *This Saving Cup*. This document was written so that parishes could use it as an insert in their Sunday bulletins. Many other articles have been devoted to this topic; for example, in 1988, Gordon Lathrop wrote an article entitled, "Chronicle: AIDS and the Cup."[11] This is a good indication that many parishes and dioceses do not offer Communion under both species on a regular basis. And yet, the documents are very clear about this:

> The sign of communion is *more complete* when given under both kinds, since in that form the sign of the eucharistic meal appears more clearly. The intention of Christ that the new and eternal covenant be ratified in his blood is better expressed, as is the relation of the eucharistic banquet to the heavenly banquet (GI, n. 240; my emphasis).

The second part of the Communion Rite that deserves attention is the practice of using reserved Eucharist at Communion time. The desire of the Council is very clear:

---

[11] *Worship* 62, no. 2 (March 1988): 161-165.

> It is most desirable that the faithful receive the
> Lord's body from hosts consecrated at the same
> Mass and that, in the instances when it is permitted,
> they share in the chalice. Then even through the
> signs communion will stand out more clearly as a
> sharing in the sacrifice actually being offered (GI, n.
> 56h).

The FDLC addressed this issue at their annual meeting in October of 1991 and passed the following position statement:

> The Eucharist and Liturgical Year Committee of the
> FDLC will compile appropriate documentation and
> provide a resource for diocesan liturgical
> commissions to assist parishes in eliminating the
> wide-spread practice of communicating the
> assembly at Mass from the reserved Sacrament.

The last part of the Communion Rite that deserves mention here is the Breaking of the Bread. Again, it is important to state the vision of the Council:

> Breaking of the bread: in apostolic times this
> gesture of Christ at the last supper gave the entire
> eucharistic action its name. This rite is not simply
> functional, but is a sign that in sharing in the one
> bread of life which is Christ we who are many are
> made one body[12] (GI, n. 56c).

Much has been written about this as well. And yet, how many of us, in our weekly Sunday liturgies, have the experience of tiny, separate wafers, that may or may not be consecrated at that liturgy? How difficult can implementation of any of these practices be? All three are tied to a deep appreciation and appropriation of symbol, something that we will address in Chapter 5. The widespread use of pre-

---

[12] This vision is based on the First Letter of Paul to the Corinthians 10:17:
"Because the loaf of bread is one, we, many though we are, are one
body, for we all partake of the one loaf."

viously consecrated hosts, Communion under only one specie, and the lack of an actual breaking of bread are indications that our engagement with liturgical symbols is less than it could be.

The continuation of these practices against the explicit wishes of the documents is a clear expression of the beleaguered hierarchical structure. The more threatened it becomes, the more it protects and clings to its power base, one manifestation of which is the Communion Rite. This may not be a conscious or intentional act, but it is one that needs to be addressed if the vision of the Council is to be fulfilled.

I would like to share two short stories with you. One illustrates the potential of the Communion Rite; the other illustrates its current problems.

When given a proper voice, the symbolic structure of the Communion Rite speaks very effectively. I was fortunate enough to attend a Sunday liturgy at a Benedictine grange not long ago. The liturgy is celebrated in an old barn; several hundred people were present and, because it was Epiphany Sunday, spirits were up and additional preparations had been made. During the Communion Rite, a solemn, reverent Breaking of the Bread was carried out. My sense is that the rite is carried out this way each week. I watched as several loaves were broken into several hundred pieces and placed in one huge, round basket of straw. It truly was God's goodness; it was bread offered; it was work of human hands; it was body of Christ, broken and poured out for each of us; it was ourselves. When we had all partaken, there was some left over. The basket was passed until there was none left. With few words, this symbolic action spoke powerfully to all who were present.

Conversely, it is easy for our symbolic structure to become broken and misunderstood. On one occasion I was participating in a weekday liturgy at a minor seminary. During weekday liturgies there, it is customary for those celebrating to gather in a circle around the altar. As we recited the Lamb of God, the presider left the circle, went to the tabernacle and removed reserved hosts, as he had probably done many times before and would, unfortunately, do many times hence. But it seemed natural enough; if there is no bread to break, the presider has no task during the Rite. I was struck by how much had been lost at that moment in terms of the meaning of the rite. Each and every time we use small, separate wafers for Communion because they are convenient, we make a choice that affects our ability to communicate. When we choose not to break bread, we eliminate the powerful symbolism of one body, *broken* and offered out of deep love for us. I was struck also by the fact that one weakened part weakens the whole. I was saddened by the fact that this had taken place in a seminary with seminarians present. Where is good role modeling in this circumstance? This does not in any way indict the presider; he is a product of his formation. It is, however, an indictment of that formation, which calls us to look at another goal of the Vatican Council that has not yet been fully realized.

Liturgical Formation

The Constitution specifically addresses the area of liturgical formation in a section entitled, "Promotion of Liturgical Instruction and Active Participation." The voices of the reform understood that formation on many levels was a key ingredient to the success of liturgical renewal. *Seven* paragraphs are devoted to this instruction (CSL, n. 14-20). Again, it is important to cite excerpts from that document:

> A prime need, therefore, is that attention be
> directed, first of all, to the liturgical formation of the
> clergy...professors...must be thoroughly trained...
> clerics shall be given a liturgical formation in their
> spiritual life...priests...are to be aided to live the
> liturgical life and to share it with the faithful
> entrusted to their care...with zeal and patience
> pastors must promote the liturgical instruction of

the faithful...by doing so, pastors will be fulfilling one of their chief duties as faithful stewards of the mysteries of God.

While much was done in terms of catechesis during the reform, it cannot be a one-time event in the lives of the faithful. We experience changes during all phases of our lives as a result of ongoing physical, emotional and spiritual development and as a result of being continually formed in God. Each celebration of worship is a new celebration, and catechesis must be ongoing so that it not only reflects the changes that we experience but also anticipates and prepares us for them as well. When directors of various diocesan offices can see no difference between Communion services and celebrations of liturgy; when bishops agree to consider promoting liturgical study in seminaries but not to updates for the already ordained; when liturgical celebrations at seminaries include practices as were cited above[13]—there is clearly a need for ongoing formation on all levels.

This discussion of all that lies ahead is by no means complete; it has not touched on the areas of music, children, cultural adaptation, proclamation of the word, homiletics, the praying of the eucharistic prayers, to mention a few. However, it has touched on some specific tasks involving the Communion Rite and the call for ongoing formation. We have also touched on some new directions that may seem too overwhelming to have any parish application:

◊ the need to recognize the importance of our bodies and the world and their intimate contribution to our worship

◊ the need to restore mystery through more attentive engagement with our symbols

---

[13] I have personally witnessed conversations involving all three circumstances.

◊ the need to update/reform the hierarchical
   structure of Church

◊ the need to change some fairly entrenched,
   harmful attitudes

The remaining chapters will continue to lay a foundation that supports and encourages change in all these areas. I believe all the areas addressed here are related to each other and I also believe that each area can be effectively addressed on a parish level. Renewal does not need to wait for a great gathering of minds, a diocesan convocation, a synod or a bishop's directive. This observation is not meant to be a pejorative assessment of these; all four can provide invaluable guidance in our renewal efforts. It is meant to encourage us to have greater faith in our own local talents and energies. We must empower each other; we must take action that continues to support the vision of Vatican II. In so doing, we allow the Christ dwelling within each of us to use our voices and our bodies to continue the visionary work that was begun with the Council.

CHAPTER 2

What Is Liturgy?

One of the goals of the liturgy is to stimulate
and sustain a deep and interior religious conversion
of the hearts of the participants. This conversion
is more than the "good feeling" one might have
after a play, for this conversion is the work of
the Spirit of Christ. — James A. Hickey[1]

I would venture to guess that if one hundred people who
were just leaving the church building after Sunday Mass
were asked what liturgy was all about, there would be one
hundred different answers. I would also venture to guess
that if the same question were put to one hundred theologians, they would return one hundred different answers
as well. It is not so much that we find ourselves in a state
of confusion (although this probably contributes some) as
much as it is that we have only just begun to articulate the
changes that began with Vatican II. This is as it should be:
God reveals Godself to us through the gift of God's only

---

[1] Hickey, *Let Us Give Thanks to the Lord our God* (Cleveland: Office for
Pastoral Ministry, 1980) in Irwin, *Liturgy, Prayer and Spirituality*, 253.
The quote concludes with: "Through him the living waters of Baptism
overflow into every aspect of our personal and communal lives."

son; this revelation moves us to worship; our experience of worship moves us to articulate and reflect upon it. But this is not a hierarchical progression that results in either a final form or doctrine; it is a cycle. Through the reflection and articulation, God is revealed anew and the process continues. It will always be dynamic. I do not believe that we will ever be in firm possession of *the* answer to the question of what liturgy is all about, but I also do not believe that this should deter us from formulating an answer that reflects where we are right now.

Why even attempt such a task? To put it in a different context for just one moment, imagine that several friends tell you that they are having trouble with *porthincia* and that they would like you to help them look at it. Maybe, by brainstorming, you can come up with some concrete ways to make it better. If you can't agree on what porthincia is, where do you begin? Is it a recipe, a skin rash, a friendship, a poorly designed piece of clothing? Do you bring a cookbook, a type of ointment, a shoulder to cry on or a needle and thread? I certainly do not want to be simplistic about liturgical renewal, but this example speaks of the reason we do need to try to define what liturgy is all about before we pursue new avenues for renewal.

An understanding of what liturgy is will help us to prepare ourselves more intentionally and will enable us all to participate more fully, whether we are assembly or designated minister within the assembly. There will always be an unconscious element to ritual participation; this is part of the mystery inherent in the process. That said, we can still become more aware of the ways God leads the assembly toward encounter with the divine to the extent that this awareness is possible. Awareness of these ways will help the assembly pay more attention to them. God's invitation to be with God requires a response from us. We can't respond to an invitation we don't see or hear. It is a process:

◊ We become more aware of the ways of ritual.

◊ We hear and see God's invitation through these ways.

◊ We answer the invitation wholeheartedly.

Defining liturgy will focus our renewal efforts and give us the means to evaluate those efforts once they are in process.

Liturgy As Ritual

In looking at what liturgy is, it is important to state that liturgy is ritual. This places liturgy into an overall structure that tells us much about the tacit and implicit rules and roles, objects and actions that shape liturgy and make it work. As might be obvious, not all ritual is Christian. Many rituals are carried out in secular context; some have observed that sports are fast becoming the new American religion. Thus, it is possible to discuss ritual without reference to Christianity and without reference to any traditional religion. We will look at a number of the more important elements of ritual here, and we will set them into Christian context.

Personal Ritual and Liturgy

First, I would like to invite you to look at how ritual unfolds and evolves in your personal life. We are often unaware that what we do in our daily routines is ritual, and, in our ignorance, we miss something vital. Children, however, are wonderfully aware of ritual. They thrive on routine and find comfort in familiar patterns. Try to tell a story to a child and leave out a line or to. Or try to change even a small part of their bed-time ritual. They will let you know in no uncertain terms how to do it right.

It is important for us to recognize our personal rituals. Recognizing that many events in our lives are ritual events brings an added dimension to them. Further, we can see that our Sunday rituals are not isolated archaic practices totally unconnected with our daily lives. The rituals in our daily lives mirror and complement the rituals of our Sunday celebrations.

This simple story might help. When my children were small, one of their favorite outings was to Grandma and Grandpa's house, four hours from our home. At a very young age, my oldest daughter knew the words to the song "Over the meadow and through the woods to grandmother's house we go" by heart. Our trips to Utica had a slight feel of pilgrimage to them.

Grandpa—my father—discovered that all three of the children loved pumpkin pie. For many years, he always had freshly baked pumpkin pie waiting for them when we arrived. Tired, hungry, thirsty and travel-worn, my children would rush to the kitchen table to see if Grandpa had made the pie. My father would let them eat pumpkin pie at all hours of the day—for breakfast, lunch, dinner, and before bed. He was a man of few words, so this pie became the oft-repeated statement of his love for my children. My children's delight was boundless; my father's enjoyment, endless.

My father died in the spring of 1989. In my own nuclear family of five, designing our own birthday dinners and desserts had become a favorite tradition. We set no rules and, as you might guess, we have come up with some wonderful family favorites (and some relatively strange concoctions even the dog wouldn't touch!). Eleven months after my father died, my daughter—much to my surprise—asked for Grandpa's pumpkin pie for her birthday dessert. Finding canned pumpkin on supermarket shelves in May is akin to climbing Mount Everest in flip flops, but find it we did. The smell of pumpkin pie soon filled every corner of our home.

Something mysterious happened that day. After we had sung and Amy had blown out the candles (they looked very odd in a pie), I began to serve the pumpkin pie. Little by little, as forks rose and fell between mouths and plates, we began to tell stories of my father. We had not really spoken of him since he had died. Our moratorium had been a silent one, guided by instinct, not by spoken word. Somehow, as we served pumpkin pie that night, we all knew that it was time to resurrect my father. We told wonderful stories and we shared great laughter that was very healing. I felt as though something heavy had been lifted from me.

Now we make pumpkin pie often, using the recipe my father used. As I flute the edges of the crust, I can see his hands—small, square palms; short, thick fingers. My hands are a smaller version. I was always amazed at how well those thick fingers could shape pie crust. As I make the filling, I think of my son who comes after me; I think of my father who came before me; I think of his mother who came before him. We were and are the piemakers in our families. At some point in the process, I will often tell my father that we are baking him in the pie once again. I feel a little foolish, yet I also find great comfort in those words. When we serve the pie, we tell stories of Grandpa. The moment is always poignant, beautiful, and touching. It is a great gift.

I see a parallel between what I now call the "Pumpkin Pie Ritual" and our Christian Eucharist ritual. Liturgy and daily life are intimately connected. My experience of many years of Christian ritual has given a depth and dimension to the Pumpkin Pie Ritual; my experience of the Pumpkin Pie Ritual has deepened my celebration of Christian ritual. I see even more clearly how Jesus is present in Eucharist and how meaningful it must have been for his early disciples to break bread in his memory.

I urge you to discover and name your own personal rituals. You will know more about ritual in that discovery and naming than any book could ever teach you because it is your own lived experience. We come to know who we

are by the stories we tell. We celebrate who we are in the
rituals we perform.

A Definition of Ritual

In classifying liturgy as ritual, it is important that we
consider these five elements, which we will look at in some
detail:

◊ Ritual is a series of appropriate, set,
  repetitive objects, actions, and words.

◊ These ritual objects, actions, and words are
  symbolic in nature.

◊ Ritual arises from a root metaphor that has
  deep meaning for all its participants.

◊ Ritual is a process of resolution.

◊ Ritual is a process of personal surrender.

A Series of Appropriate, Set, Repetitive Objects, Actions, and Words

As a series of appropriate set, repetitive objects, actions,
and words, ritual provides structure and meaning to a
gathered community. These objects, actions and words
serve to unite the community; they draw us together. We
all do and say the same things in the same way when we
gather together. Repetition allows the community to enter
into deeper and deeper levels of meaning because we do
not have to concentrate intently on what we are doing.
Repetition draws us in.

Think of learning a dance step. The same steps are
practiced and repeated each time you dance. The practice
and repetition bring grace and beauty to the movement. If
the steps were different each time you danced, you would
probably find yourself stumbling and out of sync at times.

The grace, the subtle nuances, the beauty would be lost. Your attention would be focused fully on what comes next and what is expected of you.

It is the same with ritual. I am sure that some readers can relate to the experience of attending another church where the ritual is unfamiliar and you are not quite sure what is happening. You miss some of the rhythm, energy and mystery of the ritual due to your self-consciousness and worry.

The repetition of objects, actions, and words is the foundation for effective ritual. Therefore, creating or substituting new objects, actions, and/or words in our liturgies as a way to encourage conscious, active participation might be hasty and ill-advised. In looking at renewal, we need to keep two things in mind:

◊ We must develop a healthy respect for the value of repetition.

◊ At the same time, we must balance this respect with an openness to new ideas so that creativity and vision are not stifled.

Before we move to suggest changes to any part of the ritual, the value of the change must be measured against the value of the repetition. We must also look at the ritual's meaning—do the objects, actions and words still carry that meaning? If the answer is no, we might then suggest a change, but this must be done carefully.[2]

Symbolic in Nature

In the context of ritual, these objects, actions and words assume a symbolic nature—they become "more than" ordinary; they are imbued with an energy to draw their partic-

---

[2] It may be simply that those who are gathered are unable to interact with these objects, actions, and words. We must evaluate this apparent inability. This will be addressed in greater detail in Chapter 5.

ipants into a deeper, often unconscious, level of experience and meaning. If we look at our own eucharistic
liturgy, it can be said that the whole of liturgy itself is the
symbol of God's presence with and within the assembly.
Regis Duffy has called liturgy "the presence of God calling
us to presence."[3] And while we will examine symbols
thoroughly in Chapter 5, I do not want to rush by this
statement, for it is key to our understanding of the whole
of liturgy.

◊ "The presence of God": How often do we, as
  assembly, recognize the whole of our ritual
  as symbol of the profound presence of God?
  God is present in the gathering, present in
  the elements, present in the actions, present
  in the words. The Vatican II documents are
  very specific about this. And it is not only
  the presence of God, but the presence of...

◊ "God calling us": These simple words speak
  volumes about God's love of us, desire for us
  and belonging to us as God's covenant
  people. How often God has promised never
  to leave or forget us! I think we often look at
  liturgy as something we do for God, that
  "going to church" is our gift to God. Elaine
  Ramshaw says simply that "liturgy is God's
  gift to us, an activity that God ordains out of
  a knowledge of our needs that runs deeper
  than our own self knowledge."[4] And, finally,
  ritual is not only God's presence calling us,
  but...

◊ "Calling us to presence": Liturgy is God
  calling us to be fully present. What does this

***

[3] Duffy, *Real Presence*, 3.

[4] Ramshaw, *Ritual and Pastoral Care*, 16.

mean? It means that we must be *consciously* open to, alive with, aware of God's presence. As Brother David Steindl-Rast has said, "There is no limit to wakefulness just as there is no limit to aliveness."[5] This wakefulness, this aliveness will stir and penetrate deeply into our hearts. It is through this wakefulness and aliveness that we can begin to be whole-hearted in our actions, whole-hearted in our words and thoughts, whole-hearted in our response to God's presence. In the loving presence of God, how can we be anything less? And this whole-heartedness is the well-spring from which our passion flows! While a portion of all symbolic action occurs at an unconscious level, it must begin with a *conscious assent to participation* that is alive, awake, whole-hearted. Our presence must be this conscious assent, this conscious commitment to God's presence. Once we are present, this rhythmic dance with the divine will unfold in our hearts and the potential of the ritual action will begin to be realized.

A Root Metaphor

All ritual arises from a root metaphor. This means that ritual celebrates a key event in the history of the people who gather to celebrate that event—an event that transforms and is transformed through the ritual action. In ritual, this important, transformative experience is not just remembered or talked about. *It is lived!* It is not merely a celebration of some dusty, long-ago experience but a vibrant, living action that is happening now, in our very

---

[5] Steindl-Rast, *Gratefulness,* 8.

midst.[6] Victor Turner, who has done definitive work in the area of ritual, calls this metaphor a social drama.[7] It has deep meaning for all who participate in the ritual. If we look at the root metaphor that our liturgy celebrates, the gospel of John sums it up simply:

> Yes, God so loved the world that he gave his only
> Son, that whoever believes in him may not die but
> may have eternal life (Jn 3:16).

Let us look at two points regarding the root metaphor of our Christian ritual. First, it is a living reality in our faith community. Before we organized any type of ritual, there was this reality, this experience of God loving us, loving us so much that God gave God's only Son, Jesus Christ. We can ritualize only what we have known. Jesus' disciples experienced the living, suffering, dying, and rising of their friend, brother, teacher. These were passionate experiences; one needs only look at some of the stories in the gospels to see and feel the passion![8] Even if Jesus' disciples could not understand fully, they knew on some level that they had been transformed by this gift from God. They were no longer as they had been because "God so loved the world that he gave his only Son, that whoever believes in him may not die but may have eternal life." Their limits and boundaries were broken apart by their belief in Jesus, radically broken apart. No longer was death an end of life but a transformation of it.

How did the Apostles and early Christian disciples describe this transformation? I think often of Paul's passionate statement that "I have been crucified with Christ and the

---

[6] This is often referred to as *kairos* time (as opposed to *chronos* time).

[7] Collins, *Worship: Renewal to Practice*, 67.

[8] Look at the story of Mary, Martha, and the raising of their brother, Lazarus (Jn 11:1-44); the story of the woman with the hemorrhage (Mk 5:25-34); the story of the paralytic on the mat (Mk 2:1-12), to name a few.

life I live now is not my own; Christ is living in me" (Gal 2:19-20). This is *not* a theoretical statement by any means. Paul was very direct: "Christ is living in me." He didn't say, "It's like Christ is living in me or I feel that Christ is in me." No, he said, "I have been crucified with Christ and the life I live now is not my own; Christ is living in me."

The second point is the importance of intention when we celebrate our Christian ritual. We use the objects, actions, and words of our liturgies often. The question to ask ourselves is, "At what depth?" We need to engage with these objects, actions and words with intention and passion until we feel them in the depths of our hearts. Ritual demands this.

A small aside will serve to illustrate this point. Consider the acclamation, "Alleluia!" This word comes from two Hebrew words: *halelu*, which means "praise ye," and *Jah*, a form of YHWH, which refers to God, the un-nameable. Singing the Alleluia acclamation before the Gospel, we engage in an act of praising God for the life-giving words of the good news we are about to hear. We "sing Alleluia to praise the Risen Lord who will speak in the gospel."[9] As a former member of a contemporary ensemble, I sang in front of the assembly, on one side of the sanctuary. Whether this is good liturgical practice or not is debatable but not the point to address here. This position afforded me the opportunity to see people's faces and to note their body posture. And, while most of them seemed to sing, I was continually struck by the lack of joy exhibited in this singing. Many times, it could have been a funeral dirge being sung; I cannot even use the term "acclaimed" here.

In pondering this situation, many questions arise:

◊ Why the lack of joyful acclamation,
especially at a time when we are called upon
to praise the risen Christ and to anticipate
his presence in the gospel message?

---

9 Johnson, *Word and Eucharist Handbook*, 45.

◊ Are we not in touch with what we are doing at this point?

◊ Do we lack the energy to proclaim?

◊ Do we not care?

◊ Are we embarrassed by heartfelt acclamation?

◊ Where has our passion gone?

Hopefully, these questions will stimulate conversations that lead to a greater awareness of what is being asked of us during our liturgies.

A Process of Resolution

Ritual is a drama that is and is yet to come, an already but not yet. Our liturgy is not a single event but a process of resolution; it is a process of being continually reconciled from that which separates (sin) by that which unites (Christ's saving action): "It is he who is our peace, and who made the two of us one by breaking down the barrier of hostility that kept us apart" (Eph 2:14). Victor Turner calls this process the resolution of the tension between structure, that which separates, and *communitas,* that which binds us together.

It is possible to expand on Turner's sense of resolution to include many seemingly opposite forces: light and dark, life and death, living sacrifice and heavenly banquet. Rosemary Haughton puts it very well in her book, *The Passionate God.*

> Matter and spirit, mind and body, heaven and earth,
> the everyday and the glorious—the spheres of reality
> were laid open to each other, distinct but not
> separate, interacting with the joyous perfection of
> consummated love.[10]

---

[10] Haughton, *Passionate God,* 194.

This is how we experience the love of Christ, who, as our Bridegroom, pours himself *out* for us, his Bride. He also pours himself *into* his Bride in a saving, unending action that intimately unites us together as Body of Christ. We celebrate this at every liturgy. The polarity that exists in any society finds radical resolution in this process of ritual at a deep, silent level. Through participation in our root metaphor, we are given new eyes, eyes with which to see the ultimate connectedness and unity between all. Thus, it is not so much that the polarity changes (e.g., dark does not magically become light), but our perception of it does. In the words of the Velveteen Rabbit, it doesn't happen all at once, like being wound up, but bit by bit.[11] We can see that process of resolution happening gradually throughout the gospels: disciples unsure, frightened, confused, separate and separated, gradually transformed in Jesus, into his Church, into his own Body.

A Process of Surrender

The last element we will look at in this definition of ritual is the process of surrender. All ritual involves a surrender on the part of the individual to the common value and belief that is represented in the root metaphor or drama. In ritual, no longer does the individual stand in isolation, holding fast to a set of beliefs that may contradict those of the community. Through participation in ritual, the individual surrenders any personally held beliefs that might threaten his/her community or its beliefs. We agree to surrender for a number of reasons, many of which are tied to the individual person's development. It is important to note that this surrender is made without force or coercion. This is part of the power of ritual. By itself, this process is neither good nor bad, and every community needs to examine its commonly held beliefs from time to time. Interpreted from a

---

[11] Williams, *Velveteen Rabbit.*

sociological standpoint, personal surrender brings stability and a certain "glue" to the immediate community.

The cross symbolizes the elements of resolution and surrender very well. Looking at them as symbolized by the cross will help us to more fully experience their process within a Christian context.

The vertical beam of the cross represents the process of resolution. It extends downward, drawing us more deeply into Jesus' suffering, death, and resurrection. It pulls us down into the experience of God's profound love for each of us in the gift of God's son to us. This beam pierces our hearts and makes us vulnerable to the life-giving blood of Christ. In this moment, the process of resolution is at its most profound: in the experience of a most horrible death, we are given new life. The vertical beam also symbolizes the resolution between personal and communal. Being drawn down into the inner resources of our being is an intensely personal experience. But in those inner recesses, we discover the universal and we experience solidarity with all other beings. We encounter the communal in the heart of the personal.

The horizontal beam of the cross represents the process of surrender. This beam extends outward, encouraging us to open out our arms in a posture that offers God's life to others. We are asked to surrender the need to "do our own thing" and begin to "do for others." The fruit of this surrender is a deep sense of belonging, a deep sense of commitment, a deep sense of awe. The Acts of the Apostles describes this eloquently:

> ...and fear overtook them all, for many wonders and signs were performed by the apostles. Those who believed shared all things in common (Acts 2:43-44).

This is the potential and promise of ritual celebrated with attention and intention!

Liturgy As a Weaving Process

What I would like to do now is develop a metaphor for liturgy, drawing upon the process of weaving.

Several theologians have developed various "models" as a way to describe liturgy.[12] Because it might be easy to mistake any one model as complete in itself, I prefer to use a metaphor that draws upon the process of weaving. I will use the word "threads" to describe the different functions and elements of liturgy, and I will show how we weave them all together on a "loom," which represents our process of worship.

We find our first set of threads in a description of liturgy which emphasizes its function (*what* liturgy does):

◊ sacrament (reveals God's presence)

◊ celebration (honors God)

◊ liberation (calls us to freedom)

Our second set of threads comes from another description of liturgy which emphasizes its structure or form (*how* liturgy reveals God's presence, honors God, and calls us):

◊ prayer

◊ meal

◊ story

Woven together, these threads create a beautiful fabric. Through liturgical prayer, we experience God's presence sacramentally; within the context of a meal, we celebrate special occasions and we honor guests; and through the

---

[12] James Empereur describes several models in his book, *Worship: Exploring the Sacred*, and I am indebted to him.

medium of story—most importantly the story of the Paschal Mystery—we participate in our own story of liberation.

Before continuing, it might be helpful to offer the following observations. Aidan Kavanagh makes an important distinction in liturgical theology between primary and secondary theology.[13] He says that we have become too concerned with doctrine and belief and that we have lost our ability to dialogue about the worshipping action where "something vastly mysterious transpires in the Church as it engages in worship worthy of Creation."[14] We have become more concerned with the correctness of form and word than with the wellspring from which they flow. Rosemary Haughton observes that "religious liturgy is not now, on the whole, a contact with the sacred but an external expression of a highly idealistic secular concern."[15] And Regis Duffy points out that "the Christian community may evade the needed intentions and crucial meaning of the Eucharist and settle for the comfort of familiar rituals."[16] All three are symptoms of a tendency to drift into the safety of superficiality; these are symptoms that betray a fear of letting God get too close.

Thus, where liturgy is concerned, we find ourselves in a most peculiar place: we don't talk about the process well (Kavanagh); we don't engage with it (Haughton); and we are tempted not to answer to it (Duffy). In using the metaphor of weaving to describe what liturgy is, it is essential that we not get stranded at its superficial level. It is important that we allow the mystery of all that is unseen to bring life and strength to the metaphor and draw us into deeper levels. We must allow the presence of the divine in and through each thread—each thing we "do" in liturgy—to have a voice. This divine presence must be the foundation

---

[13] Kavanagh, *On Liturgical Theology*, Chapter 5, 73-95.

[14] Ibid., 76.

[15] Haughton, *Transformation of Man*, 78.

[16] Duffy, *Real Presence*, 134.

and focal point of any description of liturgy. An appreciation of content and form is important, but their articulation
should serve God's presence as it is revealed in liturgy, not
dictate it.

Prayer and Sacrament

The first pair of threads we will weave together are those
of prayer and sacrament. Prayer is the overall context (or
structure) through which God's presence is revealed to us.
Throughout the liturgy, we are in a constant act of raising our
hearts and minds to God in praise, in thanksgiving, in sacrifice
for all that has been given to us through God's infinite love
and mercy. This is the action of prayer. "Christians are indeed
called to pray in union with each other" (CSL, n. 12). Robert
Hovda is very definite about liturgy as prayer:

> Liturgy is always and entirely prayer. Prayer is *not*
> just an element of liturgy, not just one item in a
> potpourri called liturgy. The whole thing, the whole
> celebration is common prayer. This should be
> obvious.[17]

Peter Fink is equally definite about liturgy as prayer:

> If liturgy is *not* prayer, it is not worth doing, and it
> may well be a dangerous weapon in the hands of
> those who control it.[18]

What is this action we call prayer? We began with a
familiar definition of prayer: lifting our minds and hearts to
God. In the words of William Barry, prayer is conscious
relationship, and "God does want us to be in conscious
relationship with him."[19] As we all know, relationship—be

---

[17] Hovda, *Dry Bones*, 93; my emphasis.

[18] Fink, *Worship: Praying the Sacraments*, 157.

[19] Barry, *God and You*, 13.

it with our spouse, child or God—is ongoing and requires desire, time, listening, response. To be in prayer is to be in relationship. All other meaningful elements evolve within and flow from the relationship the community establishes with God during its liturgies. It is in and through this relationship that the many aspects of God's presence are revealed. At no point during the liturgy can it cease to be relational, whether we are silent (through which we "recollect ourselves, meditate and praise God" [GI, n. 23]) or speaking or singing ("great importance should be attached to the use of singing at Mass" [GI, n. 19]). This particular thread in the fabric of liturgy is independent of any specific words, actions or objects we use in our worship. Looking at prayer, it is clear that two things are required of us: presence and participation—the stuff of relationship. At the point liturgy ceases to be relational (i.e., prayerful), it becomes empty ritual.

Imagine for a moment how you would feel if you were in conversation with a friend and the friend simply turned around and started to do something else! At the very least, you would feel perplexed; you might feel angry, insulted, embarrassed or abandoned. This imaginary experience and the feelings that arise from it are key to our understanding of what real prayer, real liturgy, is. To sit with this experience is to gain a deeper sense of the importance of presence and participation. In order to fully participate in communal prayer, its celebrants must be fully present to God and to one another. *One cannot enter relationship with absent partners.* And once the relationship has begun, we must realize that the etiquette we observe with God should be no different than the etiquette we observe with others.

During liturgy, our experience of prayer is intricately woven through our experience of sacrament. Simply speaking, it is accurate to say that all prayer is a sacrament if the prayer is faithful to this presence and participation. It is then possible to speak of the *whole* of liturgy as sacrament: within the context of liturgy we find one of the "official seven" sacraments: Eucharist. "The sacramental model of liturgical theology is presently the one most widely used."[20]

Before going further, it is important here to distinguish between what we might call "old theology" (pre-Vatican II) and "new theology" (post-Vatican II). Prior to Vatican II, sacraments were neat and tidy. Under the influence of the scholastic movement initiated by Thomas Aquinas in the twelfth century, sacraments were viewed as objects, or things, that were given out by some (this came to refer solely to those who were ordained because they were recognized as the literal bearers of Christ precisely through ordination) to others. This established an understanding of sacrament that was not relational or dynamic, but rather a sort of "magic zap" that occurred in one moment of time. (Think of the fifteen minutes that Christ was believed to reside in the body of the recipient after Communion, which, by the way, raised some difficult questions and gave rise to some interesting practices). Following Vatican II,

> the image of sacrament as "vehicle of grace
> administered by some to others" was quietly
> replaced by one which was more active and
> inclusive. Sacraments are not things at all, but lively
> expressions by the *whole* assembled church[21] of its
> faith and its mission to embody and make accessible
> the saving work of Christ."[22]

The point is that *all* those who come together to pray are equally responsible for and to the sacramental moment. We are partners, co-creators, co-heirs with God.

As sacrament, liturgy is profound encounter with God. This concept is not new nor is it unique. In the post-resurrection gospel of Matthew (28:20b), Jesus makes this promise to his disciples: "...*know that I am with you*

---

[20] Empereur, *Worship: Exploring the Sacred*, 73.

[21] Keeping in mind that the whole assembled church is made up of as few as two gathered in Jesus' name.

[22] Fink, *Worship: Praying the Sacraments*, 50; my emphasis.

always, until the end of the world!" The Vatican II documents speak of this promise in this way:

> Christ is always present in his Church, especially in
> its liturgical celebrations...every liturgical
> celebration is a sacred action surpassing all others
> (CSL, n. 7).

Liturgy is "a sacred action surpassing all others" precisely because it is an encounter with God, a revelation of God's presence. This encounter, this revelation is always an experience of grace, a sacrament in its broadest definition. The documents further state that,

> the renewal in the Eucharist of the covenant
> between the Lord and his people draws the faithful
> into the compelling love of Christ and *sets them on
> fire* (CSL, n. 10; my emphasis).

God's presence is implicit; today, it would be unusual to hear a person or community report a literal theophany—God as a burning bush (Ex 3:2) or as fire upon the mountain (Ex 19:18). Rather, it is our sacraments that reveal God and express God's presence. This act of expression demands participation; it "changes and outstrips the assembly in which it occurs."[23]

In the gospel of Matthew, Jesus promises us his presence; the Vatican Council incorporated his promise into the heart of its work; his promise is fulfilled in the midst of our prayer. We weave prayer and sacrament together in our liturgies, and we come to know God, Jesus, and the Spirit more intimately in the process.

Meal and Celebration

The second pair of threads we will weave together are those of meal and celebration. When we gather for liturgy,

---

[23] Kavanagh, *On Liturgical Theology*, 88.

we gather to celebrate within the structure of a meal. It is not uncommon to hear people refer to liturgy as "the Feast of the Heavenly Kingdom."

The first half of the liturgy prepares us to receive the invited guests into our hearts. In the Introductory Rite and the Liturgy of the Word, we make ourselves *ritually known* to one another. This "making known" is qualified by the word "ritual" in order to help us recognize the difference between an everyday greeting of "Hello, how are you?" and our entry into sacred space and relationship.[24] We often distinguish certain spaces and relationships as sacred through our attitudes of respect and reverence. This "ritual knowing" comes through the greeting and the telling of our shared story (Liturgy of the Word), our beliefs (Creed), and our concerns (Prayer of the Faithful) as we anticipate our meal together.

The entire second half of the liturgy focuses on the meal we celebrate with the gathered guests. We set the table (Preparation of the Altar), present the food (Presentation of the Gifts), prepare it and give thanks and praise to God as the compassionate and loving giver of the food (Eucharistic Prayer), and finally take and eat as Jesus commanded us at the Last Supper (Communion Rite).

So important was this meal for early Christians that they referred to "liturgy" as "the breaking of bread." While Tad Guzie speaks primarily within the context of small groups, it is also possible to experience this meal as "forgiveness, welcome and mutual acceptance, commitment to caring for others and sharing one's blessings"[25] within the Sunday assembly. Jesus intentionally chose the Passover Seder. He wanted to establish "a relationship between friends at dinner,"[26] a relationship that unfolded within the context

---

[24] Tom Driver offers some interesting observations about the function of and the connections between ritual and sacred space in *The Magic of Ritual*, 47-49.

[25] Guzie, "Reclaiming the Eucharist," *Liturgy* 7, no. 1 (Summer 1987): 32.

[26] Kavanagh, *On Liturgical Theology*, 98.

of the covenant between a loving God and God's people. No longer was our God only a God who commanded great armies and demanded blood sacrifices or a God with a long, flowing beard who sat on a throne waiting to judge and sentence. Gathered around the table, our experience of the new covenant freely emerged. We came to see our God as the one who desired to be intimately among us, who desired to break bread with us, who became one of us. This is a significant shift in the way we are able to relate to God.

One final implication of meal is our ongoing need for it. From experience, we know that we do not usually look at any meal as final—there will always be a need for sustenance, be it physical or spiritual. A good meal, celebrated in the presence of friends and family, satisfies us and leaves us in joyful anticipation of the next. Liturgy sends us forth nourished by Jesus' own self-gift, by his own willingness to become our spiritual food and drink, our meal. If we allow his example to touch us deeply, we will find the desire to do the same for others. Part of the mystery of our faith "includes God's unearned love and our enabled response to serve as Jesus did."[27] Thus, we carry our experience of being fed and our desire to become food for the world into the world and then back again—process without end.

During liturgy, our experience of meal is intricately woven through our experience of celebration. To call this simply a meal without alluding to its celebratory nature is to diminish its purpose. To define liturgy as a celebration is to highlight a very specific mood and intent through which the whole of liturgy is carried out.[28] This particular thread of liturgy has certainly been acknowledged within

---

[27] Duffy, *Real Presence,* 146.

[28] Kavanagh, *On Liturgical Theology,* 136-9. Kavanagh refers to liturgy as a social occasion and goes on to develop characteristics based on that reference. While I don't disagree, I think the use of the word "celebration" is more indicative of liveliness and spirit, both of which are desperately needed today, while still remaining true to the form of the social occasion.

liturgical circles through the movement to change terminology. We now refer to the priest of the liturgy as the presider and the assembly as the celebrants. The Vatican II documents refer to liturgy as celebration in several places (CSL, n. 7). The particular disposition of those who celebrate is one of jubilation and excitement. If we are at all in touch with the reason for the celebration, the jubilation and excitement will well up within us almost of their own accord.

We are called to be thankful for Jesus' selfless sacrifice, called to rejoice in God's infinite love and mercy, called to celebrate the presence of God and Christ in the assembly, called to praise our God for his initiative in our lives. "The feast remains its own end. The business Christians transact in liturgy is festal business because, simply, Christ has conquered death by his death."[29] Recognizing that we weave this particular thread throughout the whole of liturgy cannot help but have a positive effect on the attitude of the assembly, an effect that we must seek in the light of so many "spiritless" liturgies.

Story and Liberation

The final pair of threads we will weave together are those of story and liberation. To see liturgy as the opportunity to tell our Christian story and to then participate in it is to open the door to a much-needed sense of anticipation and enthusiasm. Andrew Greeley puts it well: "One encounters God *in the narrative, in the story* of the original encounter with God, which launched our tradition."[30] We gather (Introductory Rite); we prepare ourselves for the story (Penitential Rite); we listen to various chapters of the story, its many themes and variations (Liturgy of the Word); we

---

[29] Kavanagh, *On Liturgical Theology*, 152.

[30] Greeley, "Good Liturgy Is Little More Than a Good Weave," *National Catholic Reporter* 26, no. 21 (March 16, 1990): 12-13.

tell the story ourselves (Eucharistic Prayer); we take part in the story (Communion Rite); we are asked to become the story (Concluding Rite). This story has the potential of captivating and liberating its listeners. This will happen as we allow ourselves to be touched by the spell it weaves. The energy and gift of the story captivate us; its action and moral liberate us.

When someone asks you about one story or another, how often do you answer with the word "spellbinding?" *Spellbinding!* This is the nature of a good story. A good story also reveals something of the teller and the listener. No one remains unaffected. This is the promise and power of a good story. Our eucharistic liturgy asks us to tell, participate in, and become *the* story for all of time; we must allow ourselves to be awakened by it. This story carries more surprise, mystery and fascination than most. In this story, we are constantly surprised by God, caught up by the mystery of our salvation, fascinated by the God-man who poured out his life for us. Surprise, mystery and fascination are important elements of any good story. They wake us up and grab our attention.

We come to know who we are by the stories that we tell. The story fashions us as we fashion the story. Each telling may reveal something new or we may hear something in a way we have not heard before. This is the gift of story. And this is why a good story begs to be told over and over again. Through our Christian story, we are in a continual process of creating our identity as an Alleluia people, "transforming our vision of who we are."[31] In this story, we touch deep suffering and we also encounter deep healing. The suffering and healing flow from within the enormous heart of our loving God, "the sublime Storyteller who calls us into the passion of telling our tale."[32] We cannot help but be changed by the experience. We must make every effort at

---

[31] Kidd, "Story-Shaped Life," *Weavings,* 23.

[32] Ibid., 25.

telling, listening to, taking part in, and living out this story with the deepest fervor and love possible. We must make every effort to allow ourselves to be touched by the story, defined by the story, transformed by the story of our God who "so loved the world that he gave his only Son, that whoever believes in him may not die but may have eternal life" (Jn 3:16).

During liturgy, our experience of story is intricately woven into our experience of liberation. This story of the complete selfless giving of God to us through Jesus is the story of our liberation from all that separates us from ourselves and from each other. In other words, this is the story of our liberation from sin. It is the story of the one who comes to "bring glad tidings to the poor, to proclaim liberty to captives, recovery of sight to the blind and release to prisoners" (Lk 4:18). This thread of liturgy is about service. "It is the communal experience of the Christian call to build the kingdom which is never fully built."[33] When experienced as liberation, liturgy emphasizes inclusiveness and justice and translates the gospel message into a call for action and service. This particular thread has two different strands:

◊ It is about our own liberation through Christ's saving action.

◊ It is about our call to liberate others in loving imitation of Christ.

Our personal liberation and the liberation of others work together—we cannot be completely free until all are free, and others cannot be free until we as individuals are so as well.

The Gathering Rite forms us into the Body of Christ that we, too, might be poured out on account of others. The Liturgy of the Word challenges us with examples of God's

---

[33] Empereur, *Worship: Exploring the Sacred*, 108.

love, mercy, forgiveness and healing. The Creed strengthens us for mission through the profession of our beliefs. The Prayer of the Faithful give us a first chance to respond to God's Word by praying for those in need and praying for the conversion of those structures and people who oppress. The Liturgy of the Eucharist asks us to give great praise and thanksgiving for the story of our own liberation. The Communion Rite allows us to participate in the story as we not only witness body broken and blood poured out but partake of it as well. The Concluding Rite sends us forth to become this story of liberation of others. Liturgy asks nothing less of us than a willingness to become broken and poured out for others.[34]

As we weave this thread of liberation, we come to understand that liturgy is not about feeling good. It is not about warm fuzzies and being comforted. Liturgy is about our responsibility to the covenantal community (Church) and to its mission. Our mission is loving service based on the action of Christ who "has not come to be served but to serve...*to give his life* in ransom for the many" (Mk 10:45; my emphasis).

> "Christ's own death is the model for the kind of
> love that we must have for one another...we
> incarnate the incarnate Christ when we bring
> justice to those in need."[35]

There is an element here that is clearly prophetic and eschatological. It is prophetic in the sense that we formulate a vision of the reign of God through participation in worship; it is eschatological in the sense that this vision is powerful enough to move us to "call out for God's future reign [and] to commit ourselves to its building in the

---

[34] Hughes, "Liturgy and Justice," *Modern Liturgy* 18, no. 8, 9-11. The author describes liturgy in a similar way. She also makes some excellent points regarding oppression within the structure of liturgy itself.

[35] Empereur, *Worship: Exploring the Sacred,* 101.

present."[37] The importance of this thread to the fabric of our liturgy cannot be overstated in a world that struggles daily with oppression and poverty from varied, powerful and persistent sources.

Each thread becomes a part of the fabric that we weave when we celebrate liturgy, but none embraces it in its totality. As sacrament/prayer, the emphasis is on God's loving presence through Christ and our relationship with the divine. As celebration/meal, the emphasis is on celebrating God's gift of Christ to us, receiving the gift and partaking of it. As liberation/story, the emphasis is on the call for commitment that wells up within us as we listen to our story and incorporate its meaning into our lives and our world. Each thread contributes a life-giving image that is critical to renewal. We tap into concrete ways to help people appreciate what liturgy truly is when we can actually see ourselves as weavers: carefully weaving a relationship with God and with each other that reveals God's presence through and in both; joyfully weaving our celebrations in and through our meals together; intentionally weaving the story of our salvation in and around its message of liberation.

Discovering the unique beauty of each thread is not unlike rediscovering the beautiful, wonderfully made garment that has been hidden in a dark corner of the closet. Once it has been extracted, shaken out and revealed for what it truly is, its life is renewed and appreciated again and again. Liturgy does not need so much to be reinvented or reshaped as much as it needs to be simply taken out of the lethargic shadows that have partially hidden its innate beauty and divine presence for so long.

As we have said, each thread is incomplete by itself; each one complements the others. To leave out any one would create a hole in the fabric. Communal prayer reveals and

---

[37] Duffy, *Real Presence*, 144.

nourishes the sacramental moments in our lives. This is cause for great celebration. The life-imbuing celebration that is embodied in the meal would be empty if it were separated from the context of relationship. Most of us can recall family gatherings when Great Aunt Mary refused to speak to Uncle Henry and Cousin Margaret wouldn't speak to anyone. Broken relationships make mealtimes awkward and uncomfortable and make celebrations nearly impossible; healthy relationships are an essential element of our meal and celebration. Finally, our story leads us into a profound commitment to liberation, a commitment that will become a drudgery of "shoulds" if it is separated from the sense of celebration.

Each thread—each thing that we "do" during liturgy—strengthens all the others. As we weave prayer, sacrament, meal, celebration, story, and liberation together, we form a beautiful piece of fabric. Followed through to its logical conclusion, the fabric formed through the tireless, peaceful, contemplative weaving of our threads is the fabric of conversion. This is the underlying, universal effect that liturgy has on each and every celebrant.

Active participation in liturgy changes us! Each authentic, intentional experience of liturgy challenges us to move beyond where we are—into deeper relationship with God, into fuller celebrations of meal, into stronger commitment to serve as instruments of liberation as modeled by Christ himself.[38] Liturgy challenges us to become all that God intends us to be; asks us to discover our stuck places and move beyond them; promises to guide us into a profound act of union whereby we become the one Body of Christ through the experience of love freely given and freely received.

Liturgy is about our conversion. Every part of liturgy moves us to that point. This conversion is "a giving of love

---

[38] The words "authentic" and "intentional" are critical. Without authentic, intentional worship, we become reciters of words, untouched by the experience and its transforming potential.

[relationship], a giving of self in love [appropriation], a 'personal decision of self surrender [commitment].'"[39] God tenderly wraps us, the beloved of God, in the soft, deep folds of this fabric that we weave during every celebration. Enfolded in this fabric, we come to meet God in the heart of our very nature, in the very depth of our soul, as beings in search of transcendence, as Christians in search of their God.

[39] Walter Conn, *Christian Conversion*, 145.

CHAPTER 3

Who Are We?

...you are strangers and aliens no longer.
No, you are fellow citizens of the saints and
members of the household of God.
You form a building which rises on the foundation
of the apostles and prophets,
with Christ Jesus himself as the capstone.
Through him the whole structure is fitted together
and takes shape as a holy temple in the Lord;
in him you are being built into this temple,
to become a dwelling place
for God in the Spirit — Ephesians 2:19-22

When we come together to celebrate liturgy, we are "strangers and aliens no longer." When we pose the question, "Who are we?" we are compelled to explore three realities of our faith experience that shape our lives:

◊ Baptism

◊ Church

◊ Body of Christ

Baptism is our initiation into the household of God. This is not membership in name only; this is an active membership through which God forms us into Church. Church is far more than building and institution. We need to begin to understand that we do not *go* to church as much as we *are* Church; it is *we* who become the dwelling place for God. Lastly, we become Body of Christ through our baptism. It is a deeply mysterious transformation that happens when "two or three are gathered" (Mt 18:19). We will look at all three of these realities in this chapter.

Baptism:
Unlocking the Door and Coming Home

The practice and understanding (theology) of Baptism is, as with all sacrament and symbol, complex and one that has many levels. As Peter Fink has stated in *Worship: Praying the Sacraments,*

> sacraments aim at human transformation, a transformation that can be humanly described and humanly recognized...it is a human process...which unfolds throughout one's life.[1]

Through Baptism, we are changed, and this change is manifested in two ways:

◊ We are freed from original sin.

◊ We become members of the Church.

When we focus on infant Baptism, the first of the two changes tends to be the most obvious. The language that we use today to talk about being freed from original sin has begun to change. We have begun to look at the sin of Adam and Eve as it is told in Genesis, and tell that story in language that is appropriate and meaningful to these times.

---

[1] Fink, *Worship: Praying the Sacraments*, 11.

Sebastian Moore describes it this way: our universal first experience as human beings is that of being separated. The separation begins when we are separated from our mothers at birth. From that moment on, we experience many layers of separation: between our physical and spiritual selves, between one another, between states, between countries. Moore states that this sense of separation causes us to resist

> the impulse of the spirit to become who we truly
> are, the desired of God, the Christ. This profound
> resistance to growth is original or generic sin...[this]
> human plight [is] a condition of arrested
> development.[2]

In this description of original sin, we discover the seed that gives rise to both understandings of Baptism—in being freed from the sin, we are freed from the sense of separation from all of creation. We are able to grow together as people beloved by God, the desired of God, the Christ: "You are strangers and aliens no longer." In being freed from that sense of separation, we discover a connection to all of creation, which results in a profound and deep-seated sense of community:

> You who once were far off have been brought near
> through the blood of Christ. It is he who is our
> peace, and who made the two of us one by
> breaking down the barrier of hostility that kept us
> apart (Eph 2:13-14).

Baptism is like unlocking a door, opening it, and entering the building. As we look at our surroundings, we discover that we have come home to the heart of the God who so loves us. Baptism removes the sin (unlocks the door) and initiates us into the community (brings us home).

In looking at the two changes manifested in Baptism, it would be prudent to look at the practice of infant Baptism. It is safe to conjecture that infant Baptism in the very

---

2 Moore, *Let This Mind Be in You*, xii, 117.

beginning of the Church did not occur widely; the Second Testament does not seem to advocate it or offer detailed descriptions of such baptisms. However, a careful study of church documents reveals that the practice of baptizing infants begins very soon after that initial period of the Church. There is evidence of it by the end of the second century and, by the eighth century, it is simply assumed that the person being baptized is an infant, not an adult.

With the advent of the widespread practice of infant Baptism, the reason for Baptism becomes the removal of sin and bestowal of grace—again reminiscent of the "magic zap." We lose the sense of Baptism as the initiation into the community of faith/believers:

> If by the offense of the one man [Adam] all died,
> much more did the grace of God and the gracious
> gift of the one man, Jesus Christ, abound for all
> (Rom 5:15).

Infants are not capable of choosing to join the community of faith. Neither can they participate in a period of preparation during which they learn the history and ways of the community of which they will be a part. Thus, we are in danger of missing much of the original purpose of Baptism—becoming a vital part of a faith community.

Balancing the Purposes of Baptism

It would be (theologically) incorrect not to understand that part of the purpose of Baptism is to free us from sin. However, we must balance this understanding with the other purpose of the sacrament: through Baptism, we become members of the Church. This is why, since Vatican II, we have begun to speak of Baptism as a sacrament of initiation: through Baptism, we are initiated into—we join—a community.

With that in mind, Vatican II called for change. First, it restored the Rite of Christian Initiation of Adults (RCIA) in the Constitution on the Sacred Liturgy, notes 64-66. RCIA is the process by which children beyond the age of reason and adults join the Christian community. Second, the Council urged that parents and godparents take a more active role in infant Baptism (CSL, n. 67).

The changes set forth by Vatican II emphasize the communal aspect of Baptism: in the case of infant Baptism, the parents "make a public profession of faith on the part of the child and declare that they will continue to assist the child on the journey of faith,"[3] a journey that must be made in the company of other Christians. The parents also undergo a period of preparation that takes place within the context of the community. The entire process of the Rite of Christian Initiation is done within the context of Church (the loving faith community), who nourishes and is nourished by the ones seeking initiation. In other words, through Baptism, we become part of a community, a community whose very life arises from and is sustained through participation in the life, death and resurrection of Jesus.

This passage from Ezekiel clearly describes what we experience in Baptism:

> I will sprinkle clean water upon you to cleanse you
> from all your impurities, and from all your idols I
> will cleanse you. I will give you a new heart and
> place a new spirit within you, taking from your
> bodies your stony hearts and giving you natural
> hearts. I will put my spirit within you and make you
> live by my statutes, careful to observe my decrees.
> You shall dwell in the land which I gave your
> fathers; you shall be my people, and I will be your
> God (Ez 36:25-28).

The freedom from sin (the cleansing from impurities) is symbolized by the sprinkling of water (we need a certain amount of water to achieve cleanliness). The changes that

---

[3] Piil, "Baptism, Ministers of," *New Dictionary of Sacramental Worship*, 105.

ensue from this sprinkling are about human conversion and transformation. Again, it is important to *experience* the words of this passage so that they do not slip by unnoticed in a flurry of activity, busyness or familiarity.

It would be helpful for you to pray with this passage before continuing so that you can feel the full impact of God's words in the depth of your soul. Praying in this way involves your imagination and all your senses. Set some time aside and give yourself permission to see, to hear, to feel, to taste, to smell as you read the passage slowly.

> Feel, hear, and smell the water as God sprinkles it over you, as it cleanses you from your impurities and idols (in other words, from your sins).

> Imagine what it would be like to be given a new heart, and allow the new spirit that God places within you to breathe for you.

> Name the places in your own life where your heart feels like stone.

> Allow the properties of stone to speak to you—its hardness, its coldness, its lack of feeling, its inability to change or respond to anything, its heaviness in your chest.

> Recognize where you may be building walls with that stony heart.

> Imagine what it would be like to have that heart of stone transformed, no longer a heart of stone but a natural heart—warm, beating, full of life.

> With infinite love and wisdom, God knows that we will become God's people when the walls that we build—our experiences of sin and separation—are transformed.

> We will become one.

This passage is a very powerful experience of both changes manifested in Baptism: freedom from sin and initiation into a community that is bound to God by God's infinite love and compassion. What a profound gift!

This process *involves* us and *seeks* our assent and consent. It is only after God cleanses us and changes our hearts (converts us) that God clearly and boldly proclaims, "You shall be my people and I will be your God." The experience of conversion and of being formed into covenantal community work hand in hand with each other; it is a cooperative effort. Without community, the conversion would have no home; without cleansing and conversion, the community would have no heart.

Through our experience of Jesus' life, death and resurrection, the covenantal promise God proclaimed in Ezekiel is made new and extended to all:

> All of you who have been baptized into Christ have clothed yourselves with him. There does not exist among you Jew or Greek, slave or freeman, male or female. All are one in Christ Jesus. Furthermore, if you belong to Christ you are the descendants of Abraham, which means you inherit all that was promised (Gal 3:27-29).

In terms of our renewal efforts, we need to begin to understand that Baptism not only frees us from original sin but also that it joins us intimately to a community. For those of us who were baptized as infants (and that is probably the majority of us), we need to reflect more deeply on the significance of its sacramental action. Because it was not we who chose, but our parents or guardians, most of us have no sense of committing ourselves to a community of faith and dedicating ourselves to it; we have missed the experience of Baptism as a sacrament of initiation.

The initiating aspect of Baptism is much more obvious when we witness baptisms within the context of the Sunday assembly, when we receive the newly baptized into our midst. It is also much more obvious when we participate in Baptism as parents or godparents, or when we experience RCIA in our communities. We need to reflect on the nature of Baptism. In this way, we will understand it in its fullness, appropriate it as our experience, celebrate its grace of salvation and its gift of community. Our sense of belonging to a community called by God and made new in Jesus will be seriously compromised if we don't, and this will be, as it already has been, detrimental to our celebration of liturgy.

Church:
Community Transformed

As we shift our attention to community, we must first ask the question of how this pertains to our liturgical celebrations. Victor Turner, an anthropologist who is well known for his comprehensive studies in ritual, states that "ritual works when *communitas* has some measure of reality to support the ritual action and the ritual intent."[4] *Communitas* is the degree of bondedness that is present among the people who have come together to carry out the ritual action. *Communitas* is "an essential and generic human bond, without which there could be *no* society."[5]

When this bond is present, the ritual will work, will begin to reach toward its potential. In other words, when we pray together, tell the story and break the bread *as a community*, we will hear God's call that we be transformed and converted by God's love for us as shown through the gift of God's son. Without the support of *communitas*, the

---

[4] Collins, *Worship: Renewal to Practice*, 69.

[5] Turner, *Ritual Process*, 83, cited in Driver, *Magic of Ritual*, 160; Turner's emphasis. Driver explains in great detail and gives an excellent critique of Turner's concept of *communitas* in Chapter 8, entitled "Community."

words and actions of liturgy will be like the seeds that fall on the rocky ground—they will wither for lack of roots:

> One day a farmer went out sowing. Part of what he sowed...fell on rocky ground, where it had little soil. It sprouted at once since the soil had no depth, but when the sun rose and scorched it, it began to wither for lack of roots (Mt 13:4-6).

This is a strong and apt image. Our liturgies will wither if they are not supported by a strong sense of belonging to and bonding within the community. Many already have. The beauty and potential for growth—God's call and desire for us that we be transformed and converted—will be cut off because there is no depth to give them strength and vitality.

What tells us that this bondedness is present is the participation of the gathered group.[6] To measure this within the context of the Christian community, we ask ourselves to what extent do we experience ourselves as joined together, as woven into a whole by and through the action of the Holy Spirit? Again, this is a cycle: If bondedness encourages and builds participation, participation encourages and builds bondedness. If we do not experience the bondedness that actually forms and informs the community, we will not participate actively and intentionally. It simply will not happen. When it does not happen, a condition arises in liturgy that we aptly name spiritless, lifeless, unmoving, blah.

Moving Beyond Community

Our community is not ordinary or traditional. Its definition moves beyond traditional thinking when we use "community" to describe those who gather together to participate in a ritual. Webster defines "community" as "a

---

[6] Participation will be explored in the next chapter.

society of people having common rights and privileges, or common interests." It is often used to refer to a geographical grouping of people. Victor Turner saw a definite need to distinguish between the standard definition of community and the communities formed during ritual; this is why he chose to use the word *communitas.*[7]

Within the realm of ritual (that which we call liturgy), community is "more than." Within the realm of ritual, our Christian community becomes Church. Alexander Schmemann, in his book *For the Life of the World,* describes "the liturgy of the Eucharist...as journey or procession." He writes eloquently of this journey and, in so doing, touches upon this mysterious creation of community that happens when we gather to worship together. It would be helpful to quote at length here the words he has chosen to describe this journey:

> The journey begins when Christians leave their homes and beds. They leave, indeed, their life in this present and concrete world, and whether they have to drive fifteen miles or walk a few blocks, a sacramental act is already taking place, an act which is the very condition of everything else that is to happen. For they are now on their way to *constitute the Church,* or to be more exact, to be transformed into the Church of God. They have been individuals, some white, some black, some poor, some rich, they have been the "natural" world and a natural community....and now...they have been called to be a *new* community with a new life."[8]

We are not just a community, merely a gathered people who are bonded together or who experience *communitas,* as Victor Turner notes. We are transformed into Church—"a

---

[7] Driver, *Magic of Ritual,* 163.

[8] Schmemann, *For the Life of the World,* 27; Schmemann's emphasis.

new community with a new life." In the words of Aidan Kavanagh,

> while the church may seem little more than an
> institution like all others, it has from the beginning
> been deemed more than that because its members
> are a graced people.[9]

The word "church" comes from the Greek word *kyriakos* ("belonging to the Lord or Master"). When we gather to celebrate liturgy, we identify ourselves as belonging to God; we recognize God's promise and celebrate the grace conveyed by the promise: "you shall be my people and I will be your God."

So often we forget that it is we who are the Church, not the building dedicated or consecrated for Christian worship (EACW, n. 28).[10] "The historical problem of the church as a *place* attaining dominance over the faith community need not be repeated as long as Christians respect the primacy of the living assembly" (EACW, n. 41; emphasis in original). Not only do we confuse ourselves as "the Church" with the building that houses us, but we also confuse ourselves as "the Church" with the structure that governs us. More and more people have become disillusioned and angry with the current hierarchical, patriarchal government. To the extent that we equate this government with "the Church," we create a tremendous stumbling block for our celebrations of liturgy. Our disillusionment and anger may begin to separate us from God and from each other. Rosemary Radford Ruether addresses this issue in an article entitled, "What to do if church is an 'occasion of sin'" (see Appendix B).

---

[9] Kavanagh, *On Liturgical Theology*, 47.

[10] In speaking of Church, this note states that "it is common to use the same name to speak of the building in which those persons worship, but that use is misleading. In the words of ancient Christians, the building used for worship is called *domus ecclesiae*, 'the house of the Church'."

One more important point needs to be made regarding "the Church." Every week, we profess our faith in "one, holy, catholic, apostolic church." "One," "holy," and "apostolic" are terms with which we are all fairly familiar. How many of us understand that to be catholic is to be universal, general and all-inclusive? One current third-grade religious education series teaches children that to be catholic is to be open to the whole world. The word "catholic" comes from the Greek words *kata* ("completely") and *holos* ("whole"). The word expresses God's desire that we become completely whole—whole as persons, whole as community, one with ourselves and each other. So important is this aspect of Church that Aidan Kavanagh has gone so far as to say that "when the Church fails at being catholic, it begins to fail at being one, holy and apostolic as well."[11] This tells us a great deal about who we are called to be when we come together to pray liturgy. The ramifications for us as catholic are broad and far-reaching.

Called to be Assembly

The word in the Second Testament which has been translated as "church" is from the Greek word, *ekklesia*. Looking at the derivation of the word, it comes from the Greek, *ekkletos* ("summoned"). Again, we see God's initiative—we are a people summoned by God. We see this connection between community, Church and *ekklesia,* which is translated into English as "assembly."

Scripture identifies community with Church and assembly, especially in the letters of St. Paul.[12] This identification is not simply wordplay; it is important to liturgical renewal because we have come to refer to the liturgical gathering

---

[11] Kavanagh, *On Liturgical Theology*, 43.

[12] Gallen, "Assembly," *New Dictionary of Sacramental Worship*, 72. Gallen notes that "Paul, who is first to employ the term in the [Second] Testament, makes use of *ekklesia* sixty-five times.

as "the assembly." Understanding that the assembly is the Church and the Church is the people of God and that "Christ is always present in his Church" (CSL, n.7) is critical to all renewal efforts.[13]

The importance of the assembly to our Christian worship is noted repeatedly in the Vatican II documents, particularly in the document, Environment and Art in Catholic Worship (EACW), which is the work of the United States Bishops' Committee on the Liturgy, published in 1978. It devotes an entire section to the assembly; Section II is entitled "The Subject of Liturgical Action: The Church." A brief look at this section will help us to understand not only who we are but how we are important within worship.

> Among the symbols with which liturgy deals, none is more important than this assembly of believers (n. 28).
>
> The most powerful experience of the sacred...is found in the action of the assembly... The entire congregation is an active component. There is no audience, no passive element in the liturgical celebration. This fact alone distinguishes it from most other public assemblies (n. 29, 30).
>
> The liturgical assembly, as presented, is Church, and as Church is servant to the world. It has a commitment to be sign, witness, and instrument of the reign of God (n. 38).

These excerpts make three important points. First is the importance of the assembly. This comes through each of these notes very clearly. Kevin Irwin has observed that "to speak of the foundational element of liturgical prayer, one

---

[13] The belief that "Christ is always present in his Church" arises from the words of Jesus himself: "Wherever two or three are gathered in my name, there I am in their midst" (Mt 18:20). Because we are Church, we can now read those words as "Christ is always present in *us*." To grasp this is to grasp a significant part of the action of liturgy.

must speak of the place where all liturgy is experienced, the assembly gathered for prayer."[14] Second is the emphasis on active participation. It is not through the assembly alone that God is revealed, but through its action. It is not simply the presence of the assembly but what it does that is key.[15] And third, it is not simply the action of the assembly but its call to serve the world that is critical to the process of liturgy.

During liturgy, we must form a relationship with God, with others, and with ourselves that is *alive* with the presence of God. We must enter into the action of the liturgy and respond to its mystery with every fiber of our being. It cannot be a matter of coming into the church building, going through the motions and then leaving. This does not constitute the assembly and it will not reveal the sacred. We must be open enough to the action and free enough in our response so that we become "sign, witness and instrument in the reign of God." Liturgy does not end with the Concluding Rite. Its spirit must be breathed out upon all people in ongoing imitation of Christ:

"As the Father has sent me, so I send you."
Then [Jesus] breathed on them and said:
"Receive the Holy Spirit" (Jn 20:21-22).

This is what it means to be assembly.

Body of Christ:
Articulating the Vision

This discussion would be remiss if we did not draw out the last—and most important—reality of this assembly. In

---

[14] Irwin, *Liturgy, Prayer and Spirituality*, 94.

[15] This will be covered in the next chapter.

this becoming Church, in this act of assembling, we become Body of Christ. Bernard Cooke describes this experience eloquently:

> "Body of Christ" expresses the mystery of the church existing as a living unity whose animating principal is the Spirit breathed out in history by the risen Christ.[16]

In our Christian tradition, the experience of being Body of Christ expands the bondedness of which Victor Turner spoke. The origin of this body is described intimately in the Constitution:

> It was from the side of Christ as he slept the sleep of death upon the cross that there came forth the sublime sacrament of the whole Church (CSL, n. 5).[17]

From the body of Christ comes the Body of Christ. Like births like. The Constitution clearly identifies the assembly as the Body of Christ: "in the liturgy the whole public worship is performed by the Mystical Body of Jesus Christ, that is, by the Head and his members" (CSL, n. 7). In the documents, there is no question of the existence of this Body—"because [the liturgy] is an action of Christ the Priest and of his Body which is the Church, [it] is a sacred action surpassing all others" (CSL, n. 7). The documents don't say "if" or "when," only "because."

The documents speak of this reality as a concrete experience based on St. Paul's articulation of it. St. Paul's experience is not simply a convenient construct; it is a felt reality: "So too we, though many, are one body in Christ and individually members one of another" (Rom 12:5), and again in 1 Corinthians 12:27: "You, then, are the body of Christ." These statements describe the fulfillment of Jesus'

---

[16] Cooke, "Sacraments," *New Dictionary of Sacramental Worship*, 1120.

[17] This is the prayer after the seventh reading, Easter Vigil.

promise that not only would he be with his disciples for
always (Mt 28:20), but in them. *In* them: "The [one] who
feeds on my flesh and drinks my blood remains in me, and
I in him" (Jn 6:56).

Jesus' promise is a promise of intimacy most profound,
an intimacy that results in deep, passionate love. This love
is about belonging and acceptance. Jesus knows that he
belongs intimately to the Father and to us. His acceptance
of that belonging propels him into the heart of the Paschal
Mystery. Our belonging and acceptance is not nearly as
complete or whole. Our journey of faith leads us gradually
to the knowledge that we belong intimately to Jesus and
the Father. Our acceptance of that belonging deepens with
each celebration of Eucharist.

The communal expression of Jesus' promise that he will
dwell in us and we in him is the "Body of Christ." We are
one with Christ and with each other. We are one at last and
no union could be more complete or passionate. Rosemary
Haughton describes this process as an "Exchange" in her
book, *The Passionate God*. This deep, intimate mutual
belonging and acceptance is not easy, and there is great
reason for our resistance. Part of our resistance comes from
the fact that, as Body of Christ, we are asked to experience
not only the new life of Christ but the suffering and death
of Christ as well. As Sebastian Moore was once poignantly
told, so we must be told, "Let the drops of blood fall on our
wounded selves."[18]

Liturgy asks us to appropriate the *whole* of this reality as
our reality, personally and communally. Only when we are
able to appropriate the suffering, dying, and rising of Christ
will we be transformed by it and commit ourselves to all
that it means. As Christ has poured himself out completely
for all, as his Body, we too are called to pour ourselves out.
As Christ has risen, so we too rise with him. In this case, it
is truly an "all or nothing" proposition. As St. Paul put it, "If

---

[18] Moore, *Let This Mind Be In You*, 164.

one member suffers, all the members suffer with it; if one member is honored, all the members share its joy" (1 Cor 12:26).

It is no wonder that ritual works when we celebrate as Body of Christ. If we come to liturgy as individuals with little awareness that we are called to be Body of Christ or with little willingness to become this Body, the ritual will be weak. Period. "Perceiving ourselves as a gathering of strangers may be the biggest and most consistent obstacle to all Church renewal."[19]

Body of Christ:
Working with the Vision

The process of becoming Church/assembly/Body of Christ through Baptism has important ramifications for the entire assembly and for those involved in the designated liturgical ministries.

Liturgical Minister and Presiders

Because Vatican II placed the assembly in a position of primacy, anything that grants the liturgical ministries a special or elevated status will hinder the realization that together we form the Body of Christ. The ministries are a response to the needs of the Body and they exist to serve the assembly. If they are set apart—physically, spiritually or emotionally—they are not fully a part of the Body. This might convey a sense that the position of minister is "better" than the position of those who are in the pew:

> Different ministries in such an assembly do not
> imply "superiority" or "inferiority." Different

---

[19] Ciferni, *This Saving Cup.*

functions are necessary in the liturgy...the
recognition of different gifts...is to facilitate
worship...those who perform such ministries are
indeed servants of the assembly (EACW, n. 37).

Paul says the same thing in 1 Corinthians 12:22, "Even those members of the body which seem less important are in fact indispensable." We are all equally important, for it is the assembly who celebrates; it is the action of the assembly (the Body of Christ) that releases the gifts of the Spirit. These gifts help us appropriate the story that is and is yet to come. Our appropriation is vital; it makes possible God's transformation of us and our deepening commitment to love and serve. Liturgy is, indeed, an intimate, rhythmic dance between the assembly and the divine from beginning to end, not merely a "show" put on by presiders and liturgical ministers for the benefit of the assembly.

We must develop a greater awareness of what our local practices (praxes) say to all present. Specific questions might help you isolate areas that need to be addressed in your community:

◊ What might encourage your assembly to
    perceive liturgical ministers and presiders as
    having an elevated status, as being more
    important than the liturgy itself?

◊ Are your liturgical ministers dressed
    differently? Why?

◊ Are they seated in the sanctuary as part of
    the "chosen?" Why?

◊ Do they receive Communion under both
    species while the rest of the assembly sit and
    watch and receive under only one species?

◊ Are there other small ways in which your
    liturgical ministers are set apart, ways in

which they might inhibit the intimate action between the assembly and God?

◊ How do your liturgical ministers and presiders perceive themselves?

◊ Does your community still use the word "celebrant" to refer only to the presider?

◊ If there is no ongoing formation for your liturgical ministers and presiders, why isn't there?

All of these questions point to the place of liturgical ministers and presiders within the assembly. Their primary identity is as member of the assembly, as Body of Christ. Their secondary identity with a specific liturgical role—be it presider, lector, eucharistic minister, minister of hospitality, minister of music—should arise from their role as member of the Body of Christ. Theirs should be an attitude of mutuality and inclusiveness. At all times we must remember the words of Jesus: "The Son of Man has not come to be served, but to serve" (Mk 10:45). We must carry out our service with profound humility in the imitation of Christ.

The questions above do not pertain solely to local custom. Nor are they a matter of semantics. To continue any of the praxes alluded to in these questions is to send a clear and erroneous message to the rest of the Body: "I celebrate, you watch. I am more important than you are." This assigns the assembly the role of spectator, and the assembly finds itself detached from the drama—no longer Body of Christ fully involved in the drama, but separate and separated individuals invited to watch politely and dutifully applaud when so instructed. We become removed, and the potential of the ritual process is dramatically compromised. We must recast our models of liturgical leadership so that the primacy of the assembly is restored.

The Importance of Hospitality

Restoring the primacy of the assembly and infusing it with a new vitality must include an effort to make each and every person within the assembly feel welcome and needed. These words of Jesus describe the importance of welcoming:

> "[Those] who welcome you welcome me and those
> who welcome me welcome [the one] who sent me"
> (Mt 10:40).

When everyone who is present feels welcome, it is likely that they will celebrate the ritual more fully and completely, passionately and intentionally. "As common prayer...liturgy flourishes in a climate of hospitality: a situation in which people are comfortable with one another" (EACW, n. 11).

Generating this sense of comfort and welcome is the responsibility of all who are present: the assembly, the presider, and the hospitality ministers. Each of us can welcome the people who are next to us in the assembly; this is a matter of talk and action as well as a matter of attitude—eye contact, a smile, a nod of the head. Often, all that we need to do to welcome someone is to recognize that there is indeed someone next to us. Presiders are equally important to this ministry; it is important for them to convey to the assembly that each and every one is needed to celebrate liturgy. This, too, is often a matter of attitude rather than of specific words or actions. Hospitality ministers also have a significant role in making people feel welcome, needed, and comfortable. A warm, friendly greeting to everyone who enters will help set the tone for all that follows.

Appropriating Our Baptism

This leads us to a concluding point: fuller appropriation of our Baptism. This will help our active participation in Church/assembly/Body of Christ. "Such participation by the Christian people...is their right and duty by reason of their Baptism" (CSL, n. 14). Baptism opens the door to things of which many of us are only dimly aware. Not only do we need to help each person feel welcome and needed but we need to understand that, through our Baptism, we have joined a community of faith. Through our Baptism into Christ's suffering, death and resurrection,[20] from which *no one is excluded*, we have become,

> a chosen race, a royal priesthood, a holy nation, a people [God] claims for his own to proclaim the glorious works of the One who called you from darkness into his marvelous light. Once you were no people, but now you are God's people; once there was no mercy for you, but now you have found mercy (1 Pt 2:9-10).[21]

We will understand the gift that we are to the Body and the gift that the Body is to us when we reflect on our own Baptisms and the Baptisms we witness as members of the Body of Christ (the Church at worship). "Full, conscious, active participation in liturgical celebrations" (CSL, n. 14) will happen when we accept this gift into our hearts.

---

[20] See Rom 7:1-10.

[21] This passage from Peter is also quoted in CSL, n. 14, noted in the previous paragraph. It serves as the basis for the "Preface for Sunday in Ordinary Time I: The Paschal Mystery and the People of God."

CHAPTER 4

What Is Asked of Us?

> I feel like crying or I flush with anger:
> to be in church isn't to be calmed down,
> as some people say they get when they are at Mass.
> I'm worked up. I'm excited by being
> so close to Jesus..." — Dorothy Day[1]

Note fourteen of the Constitution on the Sacred Liturgy begins with the following sentence:

> The Church earnestly desires that all the faithful be led to that full, conscious, and active participation in liturgical celebrations called for by the very nature of the liturgy.

The note continues with this observation:

> In the reform and promotion of the liturgy, this full and active participation by all the people is the aim to be considered *before all else*. For it is the primary and indispensable source from which the faithful are to derive the true Christian spirit... (my emphasis).

---

[1] Coles, *Dorothy Day: A Radical Devotion*, 77.

"Before all else." For those of us involved in renewal, this call for "full, conscious, and active participation" has been and continues to be the goal of our efforts. In the renewal work that I have done, this phrase has been my clear, consistent guide. But it wasn't until recently that I actually stopped and asked myself, what does "full, conscious, and active participation" actually mean? Prior to that, my concept of full, conscious and active participation had been sadly simplistic. Because none of the words was beyond my understanding, I "assumed" that I knew what they all meant. A single moment of awareness and reflection resulted in the birth of many questions for which I had no answer:

◊ When do we know that all the people are participating fully, consciously and actively?

◊ How do we translate "full" in terms of participation?

◊ What does "conscious" mean?

◊ In terms of "active," does it mean that we will all pray aloud or sing with the same volume (preferably with robustness and vigor)?

◊ Or does "active" mean that we all stand, sit and kneel at the same time?

◊ How do we define or respond to "active" when the liturgy calls us to be still and silent?

The more I thought about this, the more I realized that "full, conscious and active participation" is *not* clear cut. I also realized that my own primitive assumptions simply do not apply here. While the call for full, conscious and active participation in the documents is very clear, what it means and the way to evaluate it isn't. Simply because we differ physically, our responses will never be the same. What appears to be robust and vigorous for one will be impossible to achieve for another. A decibel reading of ninety (bring along your ear plugs, please) does not indicate that participation is full, conscious and active, although everyone probably would be awake. The observation that everyone was standing when they should be or that some gesture was impeccably executed by all at the right time does not indicate full participation either. Thus, definition and assessment are difficult, but, hopefully, not impossible. To begin, we will look at each of the four words separately:

◊ "Participation" will tell us *what* we do

◊ "Full" will reveal to *what depth* we do it

◊ "Conscious" will tell us *how* we do it

◊ "Active" will describe the desired effects of participation

Participation: Taking Part

"Participation" comes from the Latin words *pars* and *partis*, meaning "part" and *capere*, meaning "to take."[2] Participation is the act of taking part or partaking, especially in the company of others. When we partake of, we have a share in that which we partake; we have some of the qualities or nature of the thing of which we are partaking. In order to fully comprehend the call for participation, we must understand what we are called to take part in and what we are called to partake of (which we discussed in the previous chapter). In terms of participation, what we take part in is the prayer of the Church, what we partake

---

[2] The definitions of "participation," "full," "conscious" and "active" are based largely on those found in *Webster's New Twentieth Century Dictionary*.

of is the meal, and how we speak of both is the story of our salvation.

Prayer

When we pray, we "take part" or participate in a relationship with God and with each other, as we are God-bearers in the assembly of believers. Participation in liturgy means that we are completely aware of the others with whom we relate. We cannot participate if we do not have a continual sense of this relationship that is with both the transcendent God and the immanent God (or the God with and within us.)

Meal

We partake of a meal that is the body and blood of the Christ. It is this Christ who poured himself out for us, who died to save us, who rose from the dead to reveal to us new life in and through himself. Through participation in this mystery, we are reminded that we have "some of the qualities and nature of that which we are partaking"—in other words, through our participation, we become body and blood of Christ. Taking part in this intimate relationship with God and each other and partaking of/becoming the Body of Christ are equally important. One without the other is not possible.

Story

In the telling of our story of taking part and partaking, we gradually realize that our story is similar to Moses'. As we encounter the divine in these stories, we encounter our burning bushes. We enter sacred space where *the* holy one reveals herself, embraces and cares for her holy ones. Out of a deep reverence and respect for these actions of God, all we can do is "remove [our] sandals from [our] feet, for the place where [we] stand is holy ground" (Ex 3:5). When we engage in the participation called for by the Vatican II documents, nothing less will happen.

Full: Rich and Abounding

The word "full" has no Latin derivative. It means "holding or containing as much as possible; rich or abounding in; having reached the greatest development or intensity; having clearness, volume, depth; ample, flowing; greatly affected by emotion; engrossed with. When we set these words into the context of liturgy, we begin to have a sense of what full participation means. No longer do we need to associate "full" with a glass of water or the feeling after a large dinner. These words add dimension to "full"; this definition describes clearly the qualities that we are asked to bring to our participation. *Full* participation points to a participation that will be deep and moving; it will be captivating to a point where we are completely caught up by its action and know nothing else for that moment. Nothing less will happen when there is a sense of fullness present.

Discussing or reflecting on these questions might give you a more solid sense of what "full" is all about:

◊ To what degree do we take part in our relationship with God and each other and partake of the body of Christ?

◊ Do we allow ourselves to do this with some depth, or do we remain on a superficial level?

◊ Do we allow ourselves to be moved and touched, or are we unmoved, separate and separated from the relationship and the Body?

◊ Do we allow ourselves to become engrossed
   and captivated by the activity, or are we
   bored and distracted?

Conscious: Aware and Awake

The word "conscious" comes from the Latin word *com*,
which means "with" and *scire*, which means "to know."
"Conscious" refers to a state "of having a feeling or knowledge of; of being aware, awake; of being aware of oneself
as a thinking being; of knowing what one is doing and
why." When we consciously participate, we are "aware" of
what we are doing; we understand what liturgy is about,
who we are as we do it. We are "awake" as we do it.

As was mentioned in Chapter 2, "there is no limit to
wakefulness."[3] This awareness and wakefulness is thus a
process, not a one-time event achieved in a single moment
of time. We are continually growing in our ability to be
aware and awake. This reveals a great deal about ourselves
and our renewal efforts. We are never finished with the
process; renewal cannot have an end. To see renewal as a
process that has a completion date is to leave growing
plants unattended.

Conscious participation assumes that we are able and
willing to be reflective about our actions, that we are able
to step back and see ourselves doing the things that we are
doing: "to know what one is doing and why." "To know
what one is doing and why" is an indication of intention.
Regis Duffy ties this sense of intention to our own degree
of presence in worship and also to the concept of honest
worship. He poses the question, "How much connection
must there be between our stories and our intention before
our rituals are honest?" He continues with the observation

---

[3] Steindl-Rast, *Gratefulness*, 14.

that "we cannot separate our intentions and our acts...we can only be responsible for our presence [and thus our participation] if we are willing to see how it is shaped by our explicit and implicit intentions [the why]."[4]

In one sense, this knowing what we are doing and why sounds very objective and to some extent calculated. I believe that, given the nature of liturgy, conscious participation also means that we be willing to accept the mystery. We will never be able to *completely* understand the action and workings of the liturgy, the "what and why." Conscious participation asks that we recognize the inherent tension here and seek a balance between the desire and need to understand the "what and why" called for by conscious participation and the knowledge that we will be unable to completely comprehend it. It asks that we become comfortable with the knowledge that our journey will never be complete, that the "what and why" will never be totally answered. This is a conscious participation that is mature.

Active: Producing Real Effects

The word "active" comes from the Latin word *agere*, which means "to act." Webster's dictionary offers fifteen synonyms for the word. Being active means "acting, functioning, working; causing action, motion, change; lively; diligent; energetic; practical; producing real effects, opposed to theoretical, ideal or speculative." Some of the synonyms include "alert, spirited, vigorous, energetic." "Active" complements "conscious"; their meanings are not the same, but they share the same condition: that of being aware, awake and alert. "Conscious" pertains more to a

---

4 Duffy, *Real Presence*, 90. In his discussion of "intentionality," Duffy refers to and quotes Rollo May's work, *Love and Will*, (New York: W. W. Norton, 1969).

condition of the intellect; "active" pertains more to the whole person.

Active participation involves the body as well as the mind and spirit. In his letter to the Colossians, the Pauline writer urges his readers that "whatever you do, work at it with your whole being" (Col 3:23a). It is difficult to conceive of something causing action or motion that does not include the body, especially because the effects of active work are real, not theoretical. Kevin Irwin notes, "When we celebrate liturgy, we do so with our whole bodies, our whole selves."[5]

When we participate in liturgy actively, something *happens*. Active participation will be demanding; it will be something that we *do*, not watch. Active participation is not a spectator sport. It is a condition that demands not only involvement (we can be relatively involved when we watch a football game, even on television, as anyone who has tried to serve dinner during a critical field goal attempt will know), but also a physical doing that is not possible when we merely watch. It must be a *doing* because it must bring about action, motion, and perhaps, most importantly, change! "The doing of [liturgy] advances one along the path of redemption provided one enters the doing deliberately and lets the doing do its thing."[6]

Involving Our Bodies in Worship

Before concluding the definition of participation, it will be helpful to ponder and reflect upon the call to involve our bodies. This is important because we have, to a large extent, lost touch with our bodies in this modern era. St. Paul pleads with the people in Corinth, "You must know that your body is a temple of the Holy Spirit, who is within...glorify God in your body" (1 Cor 6:19-20). Mary

---

[5]　Irwin, *Liturgy, Prayer, and Spirituality*, 265.

[6]　Fink, *Worship: Praying the Sacraments*, 141.

Collins has made some keen observations concerning the lack of comfort about and general distrust many of us have in terms of our bodies. Her observations might cause us to wonder how we could "glorify God in our bodies" while "negative Christian feeling about the body is in control."[7] She also observes that "we do not live now and never have lived by head alone. Ritual says this insistently because it requires the human body to articulate human and transcendent meaning."[8] This certainly supports St. Paul's observation that our bodies are temples of the Holy Spirit.

That said, let us look at one passage from Scripture that illustrates how profoundly the body can be actively involved in worship. This passage is from Nehemiah and describes the reading of the law of Moses to the people. The reading lasted from "daybreak till midday":

> ...all the people *listened attentively* to the book of the law...Ezra opened the scroll so that all the people might *see* it and as he opened it, all the people *rose*. Ezra blessed the LORD, the great God, and all the people, their *hands raised high*, answered, "Amen, amen!" Then they *bowed down and prostrated themselves* before the LORD, their faces to the ground. Ezra read plainly from the book of the law of God, interpreting it so that all could understand what was read. Then Ezra the priest-scribe said to all the people: "Today is holy to the LORD your God. Do not be sad, and do not weep"—for *all the people were weeping* as they heard the words of the law (Neh 8:3, 5-6, 8-9; my emphasis).

The picture we form in our minds as we read or listen to these words is one of great activity, of total involvement by *all* the people. First, "they listen attentively"; Ezra is sensitive to their involvement—he makes sure that they can also

---

7   Collins, *Worship: Renewal to Practice,* 108.

8   Ibid., 107.

see. The people "raise their hands" in response to the word and all say "Amen, amen!" The Scripture makes this response feel spontaneous and heartfelt. You can almost hear the words being spoken.

But the verbal response was not enough for these people, so deeply moved and involved were they. The words being read and the involvement of the people revealed the presence of God. The Lord was recognized as being in their midst and they not only bowed, but laid their bodies down, with "their faces touching the ground." It is hard not to be touched by the level of their involvement, by their lack of self-consciousness.

And "then they all wept." We are left to conjecture the reason for the weeping; sadness is mentioned, but the reason is left unsaid. We might theorize that simply being so aware of the presence of the Lord is reason enough to weep, not out of sadness but out of awe and love that are far beyond the human ability to grasp and comprehend.

This reading from Nehemiah is the first reading of the Third Sunday in Ordinary Time, Cycle C. When I hear it being proclaimed, I am struck by how differently we respond to the word today. Rarely do all the people listen attentively; rarely do all the people raise their hands at once. We reserve prostration for the rite of ordination and private moments of personal prayer. I confess to weeping occasionally during Mass, but I have never had the experience of being part of a weeping crowd, with the exception of President Kennedy's assassination, when the entire nation wept. Imagine an assembly who was so present, so actively participating that all the people recognized the presence of God in their midst, and then imagine that their response was to weep!

I believe that we have lost touch with our bodies as a vehicle of communication. Even if we sense their use as a means of communication, we are uncomfortable with that means. We use pews to separate us physically; Tom Driver offers a rather strident description of church pews:

> One of the main problems [with church
> architecture] is the presence of church pews,
> which I have long regarded as an invention of the
> Devil to keep the people of God apart.[9]

We do not always carry out our gestures with the reverence and elegance that should be accorded to them. Think for a moment about when we sign ourselves with the cross: How often are we actively aware of our bodies in the execution of this gesture? Frederick McManus quotes Romano Guardini in discussing the gesture:

> You make the sign of the Cross, and make it rightly.
> Nothing in the way of hasty waving of the hand,
> from which no one could understand what you are
> doing—no, a real sign of the Cross, slow, large, from
> forehead to breast, and from one shoulder to
> another. Don't you feel that it takes in the whole of
> you? Gather up all thoughts and feelings into this
> sign, as it goes from forehead to breast; pull yourself
> together, as it goes from shoulder to shoulder. It
> covers up the whole of you, body and soul; it
> gathers you up, dedicates you, sanctifies you...[10]

All of which Guardini speaks involves our bodies, causes motion, and changes us (dedication and sanctification).

Another case in point is the sign of peace. We often go through the motions of extending a sign of peace to one another (most of us have come a long way since we were first asked to do this), but we rarely allow ourselves to *feel in our bodies* the peace of Christ within us. If we did, our communication of that peace would be vastly different.

These examples make this point: Our liturgies lose something valuable when participation is not active; participation will not be truly active until we learn to "glorify God

---

[9] Driver, *Magic of Ritual*, 213.

[10] McManus, *Liturgical Participation*, 17, quoting Guardini, "Sacred Signs," in Martin B. Hellriegel, *The Holy Sacrifice of the Mass*, (St. Louis: PioDecimo Press, 1944), 22.

in our bodies." And that means learning to be comfortable with them, learning to involve them, learning to love them. Many of our efforts to diet and exercise, while health-related, point to this lack of comfort with ourselves as we are, as does the fascination with and proliferation of plastic surgery techniques.

In and of themselves, these techniques are neither good nor bad, and they have produced life-changing results for many. However, when we use these efforts as Band-Aids to keep us from embracing and learning to accept those lumps and bulges, droops and sags, wrinkles and spots that make us uniquely human, we need to pause and ask ourselves what is going on. When we are uncomfortable with our bodies, we certainly will not appreciate them and allow them to be a vehicle for prayer, another source of God's ongoing revelation. We will not be able to "glorify God in our bodies" if we are busy being dissatisfied with them. Full, conscious and active participation will remain a concept, never becoming a reality.

Full, conscious and active participation is thus the taking part in a relationship with a God who is both transcendent and immanent. It is the partaking of the body and blood of Christ. Participation is...

◊ an act that is deep, intense, engrossing, and emotional.

◊ an act of which we are acutely aware and about which we are acutely reflective.

◊ an act that involves the whole of us, not a theory or random speculation but a *real* act that produces a *real* effect and reveals a *real* presence.

The liturgies in which this type of participation has happened have made me cry and laugh, have rattled my cage and challenged me to look at myself and my community with a more critical eye, have engendered within the deepest part of me an awe that left me permanently changed. This full, conscious and active participation is not about feeling good, it is about meeting life head on and discovering a God who is closer to us than we are to ourselves, who is calling us to action and commitment in the midst of the motion and the commotion of our daily lives. Liturgy is life.

Types of Participation

The words "full, conscious and active" give us some sense of the disposition that we are asked to have as participants in liturgical celebrations. Another valuable way to look at participation is to look at the different types of participation in which we engage during the celebration. It would be helpful to look again at the passage from Nehemiah:

> all the people listened attentively to the book of the law...Ezra opened the scroll so that all the people might *see* it and as he opened it, all the people *rose*. Ezra blessed the LORD, the great God, and all the people, their hands raised high, answered, "Amen, amen!" Then they bowed down and prostrated themselves before the LORD, their faces to the ground. Ezra read plainly from the book of the law of God, interpreting it so that all could understand what was read. Then Ezra the priest-scribe said to all the people: "Today is holy to the LORD your God. Do not be sad, and do not weep"—for all the people were weeping as they heard the words of the law (Neh 8:3, 5-6, 8-9).

Nathan Mitchell identifies these types of participation, referring to them as levels of communication that operate during every ritual. Mitchell presents these six levels as pairs:

◊ verbal/nonverbal

◊ overt/covert

◊ interpersonal/transcendent

If we look at the passage from Nehemiah, we find all these levels at work; they each make a significant contribution to the whole action that is being described.

Verbal/Nonverbal

In terms of the verbal, we have Ezra proclaiming the word and the people responding verbally with, "Amen, amen." They assent to the law of God, they give their "yes" in the words they speak. Ezra also counsels the people, "Do not be sad." Words in all of these instances are used either to instruct, to enable response or to express feeling. The law instructs, the "amen" is the response, and Ezra is able to express a feeling of concern for the people through his counsel.

There is also a great deal of non-verbal participation: Ezra opens the scroll, the people stand, they raise their hands, they bow, they lay down, they weep. The non-verbal participation adds an important dimension to this story; without it, the story would feel quite flat and lack depth. In this particular selection, the verbal communicates the story and the response, and the non-verbal communicates the depth of the response and the feeling. Imagine the passage without one or the other and you will see the importance of both. These verbal and non-verbal levels are vehicles for active participation.

Overt/Covert

The overt/covert levels define two other types of participation. The overt level points us to the external, observable expressions of feeling and response of the gathered people or, in other words, their behavior and what happens in this story. The overt level is revealed by verbal and non-verbal communication, involving the body, mind and spirit in both cases. The overt level is about observable behaviors. We see these in Nehemiah when the people stand, when they speak, when they weep, when they raise their hands.

The behavior will often (but not always) reveal the covert level, which is about mood—how we are feeling at a given moment in time. The behavior and the mood influence and affect each other; the mood is often expressed by the behavior and the behavior often touches, supports and sometimes changes the mood. Mood and behavior work hand in hand, and communication between the levels moves in both directions. A good way to become more aware of the overt/covert levels is to ask yourself the following questions:

◊ What is happening in a particular situation? This puts you in touch with the overt.

◊ What more can I notice about a particular situation? This helps you pick up details.

◊ What is going on underneath the obvious? This puts you in touch with the covert.

Awareness of these behaviors (the overt level) and moods (the covert level) will enable *conscious* participation.

Interpersonal/Transcendent

All of our verbal/non-verbal and overt/covert levels of communication take place within the framework of the interpersonal/transcendent levels. The interpersonal level of participation points us to relationship with one another as we become Church, assembly, Body of Christ. In the passage from Nehemiah, the people who are present are referred to only by the word "all." Not once did Nehemiah refer to the people with the word "some." These people were uniquely aware of each other; they entered into an intimate relationship with each other as they stood to hear the word read. They responded to the word as one body.

The transcendent level points us to the relationship between this Church/assembly/Body of Christ and the God who is before us. This is most obvious when Nehemiah tells us that the people "prostrated themselves before the LORD." When we become aware of ourselves as Church/assembly/Body of Christ and when we become aware of the God before us, our response will be one of prostration, whether that be mentally or physically. We will be so moved. Awareness of these interpersonal and transcendent levels will enable *full* participation.

Full, conscious and active participation is the key to liturgy. This fullness, consciousness and action is lived out on all the different levels of communication. We must continue to notice and become more aware of the verbal and non-verbal ways that we communicate, the overt and covert ways, the interpersonal and transcendent. To know that we communicate on all these levels when we are in the midst of our liturgical celebrations will help us to participate more fully, more consciously, more actively. And this *is* the only way to respond to the God "who so loves us."

The Importance of Conviction

Conviction is one more important element to consider in our discussion of full, conscious, active participation. Conviction is faith in action. Conviction is the heartbeat of participation; without it, even participation that is full, conscious and active will not have the energy to lead us into deeper conversion and commitment. One might argue convincingly that full, conscious and active participation is not possible without conviction.

I would like to share two small stories to illustrate the connection between full, conscious and active participation and conviction. The first is found in Tom Driver's book, *The Magic of Ritual*. He describes a ritual called a "pig exchange" that he observed in New Guinea; the ceremony is used to settle debts in a moral, non-violent way. At the end of his description, Driver includes a bit of dialogue about what is happening at a deeper level during this settlement of debts and disputes. The following is spoken by one of the participants in the ceremony after the exchange of pigs has taken place:

> Think of this and hear this. For this change in our relationship is happening now, in front of all these people, and before your eyes and mine. When the sun goes down, all will not be the same.[11]

While we are cultures away from pig exchanges (they are probably much more civilized than the way we often choose to handle disputes), this statement demonstrates what happens when we participate in ritual with conviction. "Think of this and hear this." There is no uncertainty here, no hesitation, no desire to shy away from the effect produced by the ritual. This statement is a whole-hearted declaration. When we participate with conviction, we will experience change that happens now, in front of the entire assembly of believers. Whenever this type of participation occurs, "all will not be the same" when we leave the building that houses our Church.

In stark contrast to Driver's illustration of the importance of conviction, Regis Duffy offers the following piece, taken from John Gardner's book, *Grendel*.

> There is no conviction in the old priests' songs;
> there is only showmanship. No one in the Kingdom

---

[11] Driver, *Magic of Ritual*, 35.

> is convinced that the gods have life in them. The
> weak observe the rituals—take their hats off, put
> them on again, raise their arms, moan, intone, press
> their palms together—*but no one harbors
> unreasonable expectations.*[12]

Gone is the conviction that the ritual has life or will induce change. *Gone is the passion.* When the ritual is over, nothing has actually happened; no one is disappointed because no one has expected anything to happen. There is no intensity or emotion, no awareness, no real effects and no real presence. "No one in the Kingdom is convinced that the gods have life in them." In a way, lack of faith and conviction in our rituals is safer. When we lack faith and conviction, we will not be challenged, we will not change, we will not be drawn more deeply into the mystery of life. Faced with choosing between life and death, our lack of conviction prevents us from choosing life. Our lack of conviction prevents us from hearing God's plea to God's people:

> I have today set before you life and...death... Choose
> life, then, that you...may live by loving the LORD,
> your God, heeding [God's] voice, and holding fast
> to [God] (Dt 30:19-20).

God's revelation does require something of us: participation based upon a conviction that something important is happening in our midst and that this something brings about life-giving change that will lead us into greater life. God's revelation does require something of us: participation based upon a conviction that an important event is taking place in our midst and that this event brings about change that will lead us into greater life.

In all honesty, I wonder how many of us would have to say our liturgies parallel the example from Duffy. How

---

[12] Duffy, *Real Presence,* xi, quoting Gardner, *Grendel* (New York: Ballantine, 1972), 111; Duffy's emphasis.

much safer it is to harbor no unreasonable expectations—
and how much more unfortunate. We must begin to believe
more completely in the power of our liturgies; underlying
full, conscious and active participation must be the deep
conviction that

◊ we will experience God's revelation within
   our worship and to our community

◊ this revelation in its many forms and faces
   will leave no one unmoved, untouched,
   unchanged

◊ "when the sun goes down, all will not be the
   same"

◊ when "[we are] in Christ, [we are] a new
   creation. The old order has passed away;
   now all is new!" (2 Cor 5:17).

This is the promise and the mystery of ritual.

PART II

THE PIECES

CHAPTER 5

What Do We Use?

> ...the world itself must, in the first place,
> be known, viewed and experienced as the "symbol"
> of God, as the epiphany of God's holiness, power
> and glory—that, in other terms, it is not "Christ" or
> "God" that have to be explained in terms of this
> world and of its passing needs so as to become their
> "symbols" but, on the contrary, it is God and God
> alone that has made this world God's symbol...
> — Alexander Schmemann[1]

Every culture uses symbols to convey its deepest meanings. Wherever people gather, they use symbols. No worshipping assembly could participate actively in eucharistic liturgy and commit fully to its call if its interaction with symbols were inadequate or, in worst-case scenarios, nonexistent. As we saw in Chapter 2, liturgy, taken as a whole, is a symbol—"the presence of God calling us to presence"[2]— and it is itself made up of many symbols. It is impossible to speak of liturgy without speaking of symbols. It is impor-

---

[1] Schmemann, *For the Life of the World,* 149.

[2] Duffy, *Real Presence,* 3.

tant, therefore, to arrive at an understanding of what symbols are so that renewal builds upon a solid foundation.

In this chapter, we will look at the nature of symbols: What are their function and structure? What happens to something when it becomes symbolic? We will look at how symbols evolve in our personal lives and we examine some of the symbols we encounter in our liturgies. Finally I look at some ways we might rejuvenate these symbols as they beckon all of us, the worshipping assembly, ever more deeply into the process of commitment, conversion and transformation.

Defining "Symbol"

Definitions of the word "symbol" abound. An attempt at a complete definition needs to include a discussion of both the function and structure of symbols. In terms of function, we will look at how symbols:

◊ Indicate experiences that can no longer be perceived by our senses

◊ Bridge an outer reality to an inner reality and our present to our past and future

◊ Help us embrace the paradox inherent in our experiences

◊ Transport us to a place where conversion and transformation happen

In terms of structure, we will look at how symbols are:

◊ Multi-layered

◊ Multivalent

◊ Multi-lingual

The Function of Symbols

Let us look first at what happens when something becomes symbolic. How does the function of the object/action/word change?[3]

Indicate Experiences

When an object/action/word becomes symbolic, part of the reason is because it has begun to indicate an experience that is not externally perceived through the senses. This means that the symbol indicates an experience that can no longer be seen with the eyes or heard with the ears, felt with the hands or tasted by the mouth. The symbol serves to point to that experience; it will never be a substitute for the experience itself nor does it ever become the experience.

One critical point to make here is that the experience indicated by the symbol is one that has already happened at some level, albeit unconscious, to the person(s) using the symbol. "Symbols don't render the experience, they suggest it."[4] If you think of a finger pointing to the moon, this becomes clear. The finger is the symbol; the moon is the experience. The finger does not create the moon; the moon has been there all the time. All the finger does is point to it.

We must always keep this in mind. If we begin to think of any symbol as the experience it indicates, then we come dangerously close to creating idols of our symbols. As Kevin Irwin has observed: "Christian prayer and worship are

---

[3] In using the word "object" here, I am giving it a broad meaning that encompasses people as well as things—anything that has material substance. In using the word "action," I mean gesture as well—anything that involves motion. These three categories—object, action, word—are not meant to reduce anything or anyone to less than it is; I will use these words as basic tools with which to discuss symbols.

[4] Campbell, with Moyers, *Power of Myth*, 61.

meant to lead us to experience God; they are not substitutes for meeting the living God."[5] The manna that the Israelites ate in the desert is not the *experience* of being brought out of the desert into the promised land; it is only an *indicator* of that experience. When the Israelites ate manna, they remembered how God had tested them, how God had cared for them, how God had promised that "in the morning you shall have your fill of bread so that you may know that I, the LORD, am your God" (Ex 6:12b).

We, as Christians, are a part of that experience as well. Jesus tells us:

> "It was not Moses who gave you
> bread from the heavens;
> it is my Father who gives you
> the real heavenly bread.
> God's bread comes down from heaven
> and gives life to the world" (Jn 6:32-33).

The substance of the bread is not our salvation; it is not the bread that saves us. In the action of our Christian worship bread becomes "more than" bread. This "more than" is our salvation, the body and blood of Christ. It is the saving action of Christ in our lives: "the bread I will give is my flesh, for the life of the world" (Jn 6:51b). The use of manna indicates an experience of humanity that is common to all; it points us to the experience of God and Christ intimately and intricately involved in our lives. Through consecration, it becomes living bread, "real food" (Jn 6:55b).

Bridge an Outer Reality to an Inner Reality, and Our Present to Our Past and Future

Beyond the role of an indicator, symbols act as a bridge. A particular object, action or word resonates and connects

---

[5] Irwin, *Liturgy, Prayer and Spirituality*, 38.

the person/community experiencing it in two different ways:

◊ It connects the outer tangible reality to an inner, intangible reality.

◊ It connects us as we are in the present to those who have gone before us and to those who will come after us.

When we experience a symbol as a bridge to an inner reality and to those who have gone before us, this experience is not private, although it is personal; the bridge leads us into the universal and the communal.

If we look at the symbol of bread, we easily recognize the ways a symbol acts as a bridge. When we consume the bread-become-body of Christ, we bridge the gap between outer and inner reality: we experience Christ poured out for us and living in us; our relationship with this symbol draws us into the depths of our being. The more we come to dwell in the depths of our being, the more we come to recognize this dwelling place as a universal dwelling place, as the place where all of us encounter God.

We also experience a bridge between all that has gone before us, the present moment, and what will come; symbols draw us back in time to re-member our ancestors who came to see God revealed in their lives through the eating of the manna in the desert. The bread-become-body of Christ is a mystery which unites us in hope with all that will be through Jesus' promise to return. We remember the past, we look to the future, we rejoice in the now. And while we do this as individuals, recognizing this as a personal experience, the experience unfolds in community.

This particular facet of a symbol's function has an important ramification. Because the experience to which the symbol points is no longer a *physical* reality, the symbol needs to be strong enough, ample enough and/or well-crafted enough to actually connect us to the experience. This is not new; when Vatican II first swept into our lives and our communities, we did much experimentation with how we presented our symbols. Not everything worked, but now we seem to have settled into a sort of malaise or ennui where our symbols are concerned. We have come to settle for much less, and some of these symbols are barely recognizable as bridges to the reality toward which they point. One small wafer at communion time will have one tenth the impact for us as a worshipping community as a loaf of bread that fills our hands and is broken apart by them.

Help Us Embrace Paradox

Symbols incorporate paradox in a way that enables us to embrace the tension and drama inherent in the conflicting realities of our experience: death/life, many/one, seen/unseen, already/not yet, light/dark, riches/poverty, first/last, to name a few. Aidan Kavanagh observes that,

> symbols fold in much meaning from different levels rather than exclude it. Such discourse is necessarily paradoxical and universal without falling into contradiction or illogic.[6]

We might have a difficult time explaining to our own satisfaction how it is that Christ has come as we still also "wait in joyful hope for his coming."[7] We might have a difficult time understanding how it is that those who are first will be last (Mk 9:35), or, again, how it is that we must lose our life to preserve it (Mk 8:35). Symbols allow us to let go of the contradiction; symbols balance the tension created by the paradoxical situation and somehow hold it for us in a way that the limits of reasoning cannot.

---

[6] Kavanagh, *On Liturgical Theology*, 45.

[7] From the embolism following the Lord's Prayer.

Transport Us to a Place of Conversion and Transformation

Finally, symbols are vehicles for conversion and transformation. Symbols possess a tremendous amount of energy, an energy that transports us into the mysterious, hidden places within ourselves. They beckon us into the heart of our being, where conversion and transformation take place.

◊ Because symbols indicate an experience beyond themselves...

◊ Because symbols build bridges between what is and what has been...

◊ Because symbols hold together many different and often conflicting pieces...

...they draw us into the process of conversion. We are often reluctant to enter those deep places where we encounter God. We resist because we fear the unknown, in part because change is sometimes painful. Symbols provide us with something familiar and oftentimes comforting. This helps us let go of our resistance and embrace the conversion God desires for us. As such, symbols become the vehicles for our conversion and transformation. James Empereur sums this up nicely:

> The initial commitment which enables one to encounter the transcendent in the symbolic is only the beginning of the relationship of ever deepening commitment which gradually transforms the person."[8]

---

[8] Empereur, *Worship: Exploring the Sacred*, 42-43. The initial commitment of which Empereur speaks is our "yes"—our assent and consent—to the symbol, our willingness to enter into the relationship promised by it.

The Structure of Symbols

How does the structure of an object, action, or word change when it becomes symbolic? It develops a breadth and a depth; it speaks to us in many different languages; it requires relationship and participation in order to make it work. A symbol without participation and relationship becomes useless in the same way a car without gasoline is useless. Our participation and relationship provide the energy for the symbol; they are an integral part of its structure.

Multi-layered

Symbols are multi-layered structures, and not all of the layers are visible to the naked eye. Multi-layered structures have many levels and great depth, which enables them to indicate other levels of reality. "A symbol is like the top of an iceberg which shows above the water and shows that the rest of the iceberg is there though unseen."[9] We could also use as an example the structure of a maple tree: to the naked eye, only leaves, bark, trunk and branches are visible. Only when we cut open the tree do we see its many layers of cambium, xylem, phloem, its annular rings and, at the very center, the pith. Only when we dig into the soil do we see its roots and root hairs. So much is missed if we do not explore the "more than" which is not immediately visible to the eye.

Multivalent

Symbols are also multivalent; they express many different meanings at the same time. "Symbols and symbolic actions are capable of bearing a wealth and variety of meaning at one and the same time."[10] We do not arbitrarily assign only

---

[9] Manly and Reinhard, *Art of Praying Liturgy*, 212.

[10] Ostdiek, *Catechesis for Liturgy*, 12.

one meaning to a specific symbol to the detriment of all others. We cannot control symbols in that way. We must be open to their surprise. On one occasion, the eucharistic bread may signify Christ's body broken; on another, it may signify new life in Christ; on yet another it may represent the "work of human hands" which have cooperated with the divine gift. This ability to express many meanings lends to liturgy some of its vibrancy and vitality.

This multivalent aspect of the symbolic structure is the very thing that enables the symbol to incorporate paradox. If we look at water as a symbol, we see this clearly. Water can purify and be a sign of life. In times of flood, it can tear apart, destroy and cause death. Daniel Harrington notes that "water can refer to both the life-giving blessings of God and the evil forces opposing God's authority."[11] Somehow (in a way that is difficult to put into words), just as the function of the symbol relieves the tension inherent in paradox, so does the structure of symbols support these many, often conflicting, meanings without falling into disarray or disorder. The two work hand in hand.

Multi-lingual

Symbols are multi-lingual; they use the language of object, action and word equally well. Thus, in terms of object, we can talk of the altar as a symbol of Christ's presence—it is "more than" an object that serves as a receptacle for the chalice, paten and book. In terms of word, we can speak of the dialogue between the assembly and the presider as a symbol of their growing union—it is "more than" simple talk if we pay attention to the layers involved. In terms of action, we can talk of the sign of peace as a symbol of Christ's peace and an expression of the spirit—it is "more than" a simple handshake, hug or kiss.

---

[11] Harrington, "Baptism in Scripture," *New Dictionary of Sacramental Worship,* 83.

Relationship and Participation

The "glue" that holds the symbolic structure together is a combination of relationship and participation. If a living, working relationship is not established—between the symbol, what it symbolizes, and the people who "use" it—the symbol will simply die. It will not be a symbol anymore. When bread becomes a symbol, we see it as something "more than" bread. When Jesus took the bread at the Last Supper and said, "Do this as a remembrance of me" (Lk 22:19), he set up a relationship between himself, his disciples, and the bread. Bread becomes a life-giving substance that connects Christ's death for us to Christ's life in us. When we recognize this relationship, the bread becomes a symbol. But this is only part of the "glue" holding the symbolic structure together; it is not enough to see that several pieces are in relationship with each other.

The symbolic structure also requires participation; it requires response. We spoke of this earlier as our saying "yes" to the symbol. This assent is important enough to reiterate. Liturgical symbols must be actively engaged in if they are to be realized symbols and not just potential symbols.[12] We can recognize the many aspects of relationship being revealed between God and God's people during our liturgies without ever participating in them. We can look, detach ourselves from the action, lean back and say, "That's interesting" or worse, "This doesn't pertain to me" and never participate in what is happening around us. When we do not engage wholeheartedly with our symbols, the potential for passion, vitality, vibrancy—the potential for liturgy and life to be one continuous act of a gracious God and God's grateful people—dies even before it is born. Participation is the beating heart of symbolic life.

---

[12] Skublics, "Psychologically Living Symbolism and Liturgy," *Carl Jung and Christian Spirituality*, 216.

The Mystery of Symbols

One final point in our effort to define "symbol" involves their ineffable aspects. No symbol will ever be fully known or fully defined; we must learn to accept its mystery and learn to dwell comfortably within its veiled structure. "Because the symbol involves a one-to-many relationship it resists translation or explanation."[13] And while we have explored many aspects of symbols, this aspect of mystery is perhaps the most important. We must always understand that we can never know all there is to know about the process. Much of it remains out of our grasp; a mature approach to symbols respects and values this as its source of energy and transformation.

Thus, to now take each of our liturgical symbols and subject it to a linear, intellectual analysis would be a mistake. While it will be helpful to look at our Christian symbols, to do this in as deliberate and determined a manner as possible is to dishonor the symbol. This type of analysis does not serve the delicate, intricate nature of symbols; it obliterates it. Imagine, if you will, being in a dark room where the narrowest beam of light appears to guide you in your journey. In your attempt to find out all you can about this mysterious beam of light, you turn on an overhead light so that you can see it better. Once that overhead light floods the room, the narrow beam is lost and it is no longer able to guide you.

Compulsive explanation can do this to symbols. Ernest Skublics notes that "every pretense or even innocent conviction that we know everything the symbol means spells death to the symbol."[14] Again, this process of understanding is a delicate one. It would be foolish to say unequivocally that an understanding or description of a

---

[13] Empereur, *Worship: Exploring the Sacred*, 41.

[14] Skublics, "Psychologically Living Symbolism and Liturgy," *Carl Jung and Christian Spirituality*, 216.

particular symbol is not useful or helpful. It is. But, it is important to point out again that this process must be balanced by the willingness to allow the symbol to retain its mystery, to respect its veiled structure. This is part of its energy and allure.

Recognizing Personal Symbols

Before we apply what we now know about symbols to our liturgical experience, let us first look at symbols from the standpoint of personal experience. A meaningful symbol reveals a process that has a tremendous amount of energy, an energy that transforms us. I firmly believe that we must say "yes" to these symbols if we are to tap into their energy, if we are to experience them with depth.

Symbols are extraordinary tools. We make a choice each time we encounter them; we can choose to relate to them and, in so doing, give them the voice they need to speak to us. In doing so, we set free the abundant life that lies within each one.

That said, we can make a second choice. We can decide to use a symbol at face value, as an object and not a process, as a curiosity outside of ourselves and not as an experience related to and pointing toward our innermost being. This is a safe choice, one that has been made often enough to leave us questioning whether our symbols have become bankrupt and meaningless. My sense is that they have not. My sense is that we have simply chosen too many times to remain on an external level when we use them. We have chosen to *use* them as *objects* that have no depth, that have no greater meaning or purpose. This is a great travesty. I would like to share with you two stories about the evolution of something I have come to name "personal" symbols. The symbols are full of energy (they are very powerful); naming them has helped me to understand the symbolic process in a very intimate way.

Forsythia Bushes and Pinecones

In May of 1977, our first child was born. My husband and I had looked forward to this event for a long time. Because we had been married for five years, we had had a great deal of time to anticipate, dream and plan for children. Pregnancy and birth were blessed events for all of us; I experienced good health throughout and Amy was born with no complications.

The day we brought her home from the hospital was one of those cool, gorgeous, quintessential spring days in New England that have no equal. It was bright and breezy, the sky was a deep blue with no clouds visible for as far as the eye could see. The ten-mile trip home in our little green Volkswagon Rabbit was one of those "I-can't-wait-to-get-home-but-what-do-we-do-once-we-are-there-with-this-new-little-creature" trips, full of excitement and full of nervousness. The forsythia along the banks of the highway was in full bloom, a brilliant yellow as I had never seen before and have never seen again. In the breeze, the heavily-laden boughs moved slowly and gracefully, protesting the urgings of the wind. In the promising spring sunshine, the tiny yellow blossoms possessed a brilliance and a sparkle that was breathtaking.

I have never felt the same about forsythia since. There has always been a "special something" surrounding it that I have been at a loss to explain. It is only in doing all this work with symbolism in the last several years that I have begun to understand this special something. When I encounter forsythia in full bloom, I can be mysteriously transported back to that morning in that little green Rabbit, driving home for the very first time with our first-born child carefully wrapped in blanket and safely secured in car seat. It is "more than" simply remembering; I am *living* it in a powerful way. The forsythia represents to me a myriad of emotions and feelings, a myriad of experiences and messages that I have not yet been able to articulate fully to my own satisfaction even now, many years after the initial event. The forsythia has become for me a story of new life and endless possibility, a story of dreams and promises, a story that is exciting and scary all at once, a story of love between a parent and a child that is just beginning and yet has somehow always been there.

When I see forsythia in full bloom, I can choose to tap into the energy that it now has for me or I can continue on my way, composing grocery lists in my head or planning our next vacation, whatever might be on my mind at that moment. I know I can choose to do this because I have. Or I can choose to stop and allow the mysterious relationship that has developed between us to draw me into its depths, to enfold me in its story. While this may sound deliberate, it isn't always so conscious or so calculated. At times, I am so caught up with some thought that I don't even see the forsythia. At other times, before I even realize it, the forsythia has transported me back to that incredible morning. Through the dynamics of this relationship, both the forsythia and I become "more than" we are.

For readers who may have trouble relating to birth and babies, perhaps another story might encourage you or help you to find and relate to a personal symbol.

My second "personal" symbol is that of a simple pinecone, perhaps an inch tall and a half-inch in circumference. This pinecone is over twenty years old and comes from the first Christmas tree that I had as an adult, married woman. This was in the early seventies when we were living in Colorado. Each December, national forest land was opened to the public, and certain evergreen trees were tagged for removal for a small fee of five dollars.

Because of the normally heavy early snows in the region, four-wheel-drive vehicles were a standard requirement. However, this particular year was a dry one and there had not been a significant snowfall in the area, so even regular cars were allowed. We were living on an extremely tight budget, so the idea of a five-dollar Christmas tree was a welcome one. Few trees were left by the time we got to the area, but there was one sad, small little tree with two trunks that was leaning somewhat pathetically into the small rise of a hill. We chose this one after much discussion, in part because we were impossible romantics and in part because there was something endearing about it, even though it wasn't the "perfect tree." It never did stand up straight, but enough decorations, lights and tinsel lent some saving graces to it. There was one small pinecone attached to the top of the tree. I carefully detached this pinecone from its growing place and saved it; it has been a part of every Christmas tree since that first one.

I anticipate this seed every year. I hold it in my hand as we carefully unwrap our ornaments and there is the feel of ceremony in the act. I live again that moment in time so many years ago, a moment that has come to mean (or symbolize) surprise (after all, we had never expected that we would be allowed into the forest in our old, sometimes-reliable '63 Chevy); a moment that has come to mean riches in the face of near poverty; a moment that has come to mean beauty where we initially saw only defect; a moment that has come to mean youth and simplicity. Again, it is impossible to tell the story myself; it is the story of a wordless relationship that exists between the pinecone and me. The pinecone has an energy that seeks only my willingness to listen so that it can speak its language of mystery and magic. It is far "more than" a small pinecone. It is like a prism that you hold up to the light—as you turn it slowly, endless colors and patterns reflect against the wall. The more it is turned, the more the many faces of light are revealed.

I share these stories for two reasons: first, to illustrate the energy (or power) of symbol; second, to illustrate the choice that we often have in terms of relating to that symbol. We all have personal symbols; we may not have labeled them as such (the forsythia and the pinecone were mine long before they were labeled as such), but we have them, nonetheless. To intellectually understand the symbolic process is necessary; to understand it from the realm of personal experience is equally so. Both understandings are needed to build a balanced, solid framework that is not only conceptual but also experiential. I would urge you to search out your own personal symbols and spend time with them—empower them, give them a proper voice and allow them to tell you their story. Most importantly, open yourself to their energy, feel that energy and become aware of your role in the unfolding of their story and the release of their energy. Ernest Skublics describes our relationship with symbols:

> the role of perception, or better, communication,
> incarnational participation, involvement, is
> obviously crucial to the vitality of the symbol...if not
> engaged in...it cannot possibly be a real symbol for
> the person in question.[15]

Without conscious attention on your part, your personal symbols will never tell their story, never release their energy, never begin to meet their potential for drawing you into the very depths of life that is at one and the same time particular and universal. Identifying and reflecting on your personal symbols will be as valuable and revealing as any intellectual, academic discussion and will serve to balance that discussion.

Once we have touched our own personal symbols, it is a simple step to transfer that process to our communal liturgical symbols. These symbols bear as much energy as do our personal ones; they require every bit as much attention, willingness and assent as our personal ones do. We need to name our primary liturgical symbols and then begin to work with those symbols in a way that is experiential and reflective, in a way that helps us touch and enter the depth of our collective soul. Robert Hovda tells us that "primary symbols must be identified and distinguished, so

---

[15] Skublics, "Psychologically Living Symbolism and Liturgy," *Carl Jung and Christian Spirituality*, 216.

that the message of Jesus and reconciliation is not lost in a crowd of peripheral figures."[16]

Exploring Liturgical Symbols

As stated earlier, symbols speak many different languages; object, action and word are their primary vehicles of expression. The document Environment and Art in Catholic Worship states that "it is important to focus on central symbols and to allow them to be expressed with full depth of their vision" (n. 87).

In terms of objects, some of these symbols include bread and wine, water, cross, candles, altar, lectionary and Book of Gospels, people, presider, vestments.

In terms of action, some of these symbols include the gathering of the assembly; the procession of the liturgical ministers; the making of the sign of the cross; the incensing of the sacred texts, gifts and people; the proclamation of the word; the Presentation of the Gifts; the consecration of the gifts; the breaking of the bread; the giving of peace; the partaking of the one body and blood; the sending forth.

In terms of spoken and sung word, some of these symbols include single words; dialogue between assembly and presider; prayers of praise, thanksgiving and petition; statements of belief; acclamations, which are normally sung; and Scripture, which is read and sung.

All of these are a part of external reality, a reality that is concrete and involves the senses: they can be either seen or heard, touched or felt, smelled or tasted.

Many of these symbols predate the Christian era, such as bread and wine, altar, sacred books, gathering, proclamation, presentation, spoken and sung word. Some arise directly from the disciples' experiences with Jesus, includ-

---

[16] Hovda, *Dry Bones*, 78.

ing the sign of the cross, the consecration, the giving of peace, the partaking of the body and blood, the sending forth. Like personal symbols, all of these arise from real experiences that took place at a specific moment in time. Within the context of a faith community, we live these experiences in the present moment when we celebrate liturgy together.

All of these symbols can be traced to Scripture. We need merely to reflect on the passage from Nehemiah that we used in Chapter 4 to see the importance of sacred books, the gathering and the proclamation. These objects and actions become "more than" because they arise from and represent a significant experience of a faith community; they are important enough to become a part of its ritual life because they reveal God. We can see how bread becomes symbolic from the ancient Exodus story of the manna in the desert (Ex 16:4). It becomes "more than" food; it becomes a symbol of God's presence and providence to God's people. The breaking of bread, the giving of peace and the sending forth are taken directly from the gospels.

It would take an entire book to look at each and every liturgical symbol. We have mentioned many already: liturgy as a symbol of God's presence calling us to presence; the cross as a symbol of the Paschal Mystery, which we personally appropriate and to which we commit ourselves; assembly as a symbol of Body of Christ and revelation of the sacred; water as a symbol of life and instrument of destruction; eucharistic bread as a symbol of many things on many levels. The explanation of what each of these symbolizes has been brief. Again, there is a struggle in knowing when the explanation is enough and when it is so dogged that it has violated the mystery. The purpose of any explanation is to awaken ourselves to the experience beckoning in each. Its purpose also is to give each symbol a tiny voice, a whisper really, that speaks gently and delicately in the silence of our hearts and invites us into deeper layers of our being where God's presence illuminates our darkness.

Symbols are based upon the real, felt experience of real people—experience that reveals in some way or form a God who is among/with/within them. This is what we are called to experience when we relate to symbols. The evolution of our liturgical symbols is not an arbitrary process that makes use of objects, actions and words that we choose simply because they are convenient to use or because they are something we happen to have on hand. I could not decide to substitute a lilac bush for the forsythia any more easily than our community of faith could choose to substitute graham crackers for bread in our eucharistic celebration. We must respect the origin of our symbols and encourage participation with them.

By becoming more aware of the function and structure of symbols, we are initiating dialogue with our Christian symbols. This dialogue begins when a symbol attracts us and holds our attention, when it becomes "more than" simply bread, "more than" two pieces of wood bound or nailed together in the shape of a "†". Return to the image of a whisper in the chamber of our hearts, "Come back to me with all your heart." In the silence, the whisper becomes a mighty roar that is difficult to resist. We answer spontaneously and with a certain amount of surprise, "We are here. Your energy captivates us! We can feel ourselves being drawn toward something; we can't explain it and we really don't understand." While we may never have a conversation with a symbol—it sounds awkward and a bit foolish—this is what happens in the inner recesses of our hearts when we begin to notice.

It might be helpful to look at two symbols—one word and one action—to get a fuller sense of how to listen, follow, and respond to the level and meaning of the symbol as it speaks to us on a given day, in a given moment. It may be different each time we enter the dialogue. We must open ourselves to the possibility of continual surprise.

Symbolic Word: "Amen"

"Amen," on the surface (the tip of the iceberg, the bark of the tree), is a response to the prayers of the assembly, the presider, and the words of Scripture. As an assembly, we speak it frequently. Structurally, because it is said at the end of these prayers, it is not only a response, but a conclusion as well. Perhaps because it is a frequent response, perhaps because of its brevity, it often slips by without even a nod of our heads. And yet, each "amen" that we say carries tremendous potential within it.

If we study the word for just a moment, we can see how it serves to unite us to the presider; it makes the prayers he prays ours as well as his: "By their acclamation, Amen, the people make the prayer their own" (GI, n. 56k).[17] The amen "is the symbol of community involvement in Christian life and worship."[18] Not only is it the climax to our prayers, it is our way of saying "yes" to God in a deep, definitive, intentional way. St. Augustine has often been quoted: "Your Amen, my [brothers and sisters], is your signature, your assent, your affirmation." It is the signature of a Christian, an assent to the God who is before us, a recognition of God's love for us.

The experience and the impact of this word cannot be overestimated or overstated. In one instance, we may be deeply aware of the unity of all believers as we utter the word; in another, we may be aware of the personal commitment we make when we say the word; in yet another, there may be no intellectual awareness, simply a feeling that resonates in every fiber of our being, a resonance that is moving enough to bring tears to our eyes. In each case, we are being led more deeply into the heart of our God

---

[17] The "Amen" to which the General Instruction refers in this instance is at the end of the prayer after communion.

[18] Empereur, *Worship: Exploring the Sacred*, 11.

who so loves us. This is the holy process of Christian symbolism.

Symbolic Action: Sign of the Cross

In Chapter 4, we looked at Romano Guardini's description of the physical motion that constitutes making the sign of the cross.[19] In one instance, we may experience it as a dedication of ourselves to God; in another, as our sanctification. In yet another, we experience the making of the sign of the cross as a symbol of our unity. The Vatican documents mention that when we uniformly do something, the action serves to unite us all:

> The uniformity in standing, kneeling, or sitting to be observed by all taking part is a sign of the community and the unity of the assembly; it both expresses and fosters the spiritual attitude of those taking part (GI, n. 20).

In the eyes of my then six-year-old daughter, the sign of the cross has yet another meaning. One day we were discussing the meaningful matters of life as only six year olds can do with an innocence that is touching and a wisdom that belies their age. She looked up at me with her blue eyes wide open and said, "Mommy, I know what the sign of the cross is; it's God's telephone number." It is one of the few moments of my life when I have found myself at a loss for words! We gather together as community, as Body of Christ, and our first action together is to call out to God, to make contact with the holy one who has made us a holy people, loved and desired by God. My daughter's insight has opened my eyes and deepened my appreciation of this simple symbolic action.

---

[19] It would be worthwhile to reread this passage, found on page 95, in light of its symbolic significance.

Assessing Ourselves and Our Symbols

After all that we have said about the wondrous, mysterious function of symbol, it might now be clear that those we encounter during liturgy today are not engaging us fully. A careful observation of the current state of liturgy in your community might support the following assessment:

◊ little heartfelt commitment

◊ waning *selfless* service

◊ little experience of *lasting* conversion[20]

Many of us are card-carrying Catholics in search of a quick fix. We are not willing to enter into the depth and breadth inherent in our symbols. Thus they are becoming largely ineffective and will eventually die to their original purpose and meaning. Regis Duffy comments that,

> ...if we go through the external motions of symbols but do not appropriate their challenging meaning, then our symbols are reduced to signs and our communication becomes distorted.[21]

Joseph Campbell says this in another way, speaking of every religion as being true "when understood metaphorically. But when it gets stuck to its own metaphors, interpreting them as facts, then you are in trouble."[22]

Thus, it would be a mistake to conclude that our liturgical symbols are dead, obsolete or meaningless. What both Duffy and Campbell allude to is the incomplete way we relate to them, not to actual faults in the symbols themselves. We, as a Western culture, have lost our ability to

---

[20] Conversion will be discussed more comprehensively in the next chapter.

[21] Duffy, *Real Presence*, 17.

[22] Campbell, with Moyers, *Power of Myth*, 56.

communicate in a symbolic way. We are not able to experience symbols as relational, participatory and fully alive. We do not hear our symbols calling us to a deeper level of meaning and way of being that, in the Christian context, is more consistent with the gospel message.

To recognize that our symbols are largely ineffective is a vital first step. It would be premature, however, to propose that we to modify or drop long-standing symbols and attempt to create new ones.[23] Again, we need to exercise common sense here; we can err on either side. If we cling too tightly to the way things are simply because "we have always done it this way," then we will create a rigid, inflexible system that has little vitality and imagination. If we decide to try anything once, without careful discrimination, we will bring about chaos and confusion.

Mary Collins has argued convincingly that some symbols have, indeed, been rendered obsolete. In a study of the rite of profession for Benedictine women, she discovered that a number of symbols traditionally associated with the rite had been eliminated because they no longer held any meaning for the community.[24] What this points to is a need for some type of ongoing evaluation of our rituals: liturgy is a catalyst for our change; it calls us to be transformed ever more deeply into Christ. But this is not a one-directional process. We become the catalyst for liturgy as well, as the Vatican Council II so aptly became. As we are called into the process of conversion through the symbolic action of the liturgy, we are also called to "interpret and elaborate the received tradition [in this case, our liturgy] as we participate in it."[25]

Mary Collins' study also points out a need to name our primary symbols, respect their primacy, and open them up

---

[23] However, Joseph Campbell, in the *Power of Myth*, page 18, does make a convincing argument for creating new symbols and myths.

[24] Collins, *Worship: Renewal to Practice*, 95-6.

[25] Ibid., 97.

"until we can experience all of them as authentic and appreciate their symbolic value" (EACW, n. 15). The very nature of our primary symbols defies manipulation, reinterpretation, substitution. There is a transcendent quality to certain of our symbols. These symbols are so central to our faith experience that they are not tied to a particular set of cultural conditions or qualifications. They arise out of timeless, universal experiences that touch all human beings. In the Second Testament, Jesus repeatedly uses the symbols of bread and wine, water, fire, cross, darkness and light, sacred word, covenant community. He refers many times to the symbolic actions of blessing and breaking, giving and receiving, dying and rising. The stories in the Second Testament echo and build upon the stories and experiences of the First Testament; the deliberate linking of the two unites all of us as one faith community: "There does not exist among you Jew or Greek, slave or freeman, male or female. All are one in Christ Jesus" (Gal 3:28).

Jesus knows these symbols are important to us. He knows they unite us because they are universal; on some level, they are a part of everyone's experience. That is why he uses them. The forsythia bush and pinecone will forever be my own personal symbols—they do not carry a deep meaning for every person. But the symbols of bread and wine, etc., are an intimate part of the broader experience of being human. We cannot change them simply because we are frustrated by the lack of response in our liturgies. We must begin to understand and accept this. We must recognize that the energy and life stored in our primary symbols are not accidents. They rely on experiences that reside in all of us by virtue of our humanity.[26]

---

[26] Progoff, "Waking Dream and Living Myth," *Myths, Dreams and Religion,* 180. The author discusses this particular aspect of the nature of symbolism. He refers more formally to this phenomenon as the collective, objective unconscious. The entire article is particularly well done and has interesting implications and parallels for liturgy.

Arbitrary duplication or change is an easy way out. As the bridge to these universal experiences, symbols have the ability to unite us to all other creatures because they lead us into a fuller awareness of our commonality.

> It is through our very commonness, rather than our individual uniqueness, that we and Christ are linked...what is written to the Corinthians is valid twenty centuries later.[27]

This sense of oneness at the core of being that is indicated by and mediated through symbols is unchanging, universal, timeless, unitive. To embark on the development of new (if that is even possible, given the way symbols evolve and work) or modernization of existing symbols would, therefore, be a difficult undertaking with questionable outcome. It seems practical to examine what we already have and enable them to blossom into their full potential before we look at other solutions.

Rejuvenating Our Liturgical Symbols

So what can be done? How do we examine what we have? How do we help our symbols be symbols and reach their potential as that which reveals God in God's many ways?

First, we need to begin with a basic understanding and awareness of what a symbol is. This is like the knocking at the door. If we do not hear the knock at the door, we will not go to the door to let in the person knocking. It is difficult to participate in something if that something is not perceived or sensed. Teaching about symbols in a general way teaches people to listen for the knock. This is not to say that we dissect each and every liturgical symbol and offer every possible explanation and meaning for these

---

[27] Searle, Mark. "Liturgical Prayer Today." *Studies in Formative Spirituality* 3 (November 1982): 404-5.

symbols. We know from our previous discussion that this will not work. It might make the teachers feel as though they have accomplished a great deal and done a good job when, in effect, this type of exposure deadens the symbols.

Second, we must help people open the door when they hear the knock. Opening the door is opening ourselves to relationship and participation. We open ourselves to experiences/encounters with our liturgical symbols that are not solely verbal and intellectual exercises. After all, "liturgy is a symbol—*not* to be explained, for that would be more of a hindrance than a help, but to be experienced."[28] Because symbols nearly defy cogent explanation, the best that can be hoped for in their exploration is that they be more deeply brought to life and more broadly felt in a way that awakens our intuitive and internal processes. The task is a delicate one. This process must continue to incorporate and accept an unconscious element; no symbol will ever be completely explained.

What might this process look like in your community setting? You might gather together for an evening of prayer and select a particular liturgical symbol as your focus for the evening. One evening, you might select the altar and altar stone. The following process might will work well:

◊ Listen to various Scripture passages that mention altar and stone.

◊ Pray with these passages quietly.

◊ Share your reflections about the Scripture together.

◊ Gather around the altar for several minutes of silent contemplation.

◊ Involve your whole bodies: incense the altar, then invite each person to reverence it, as

---

[28] Manly and Reinhard, *Art of Praying Liturgy*, 217.

the presider does at the beginning of each
liturgy.

◊ Close the evening with a prayer of
thanksgiving for all that God has given to us
out of God's great love for us.

This type of evening touches people on many levels and
gives the chosen symbol an opportunity to tell its story,
personally and communally. It involves your bodies
through sound (as you listen to the Scriptures proclaimed),
through sight (as you gather around the altar to pray),
through smell (as you incense the altar), through touch (as
you reverence the altar). It involves you personally as you
each hear the Scripture and then reflect on it in the silence
of your hearts; it involves you communally as you share
your reflections and pray together. It involves you emotionally and spiritually.

When you gather again for liturgy, your experience of the
altar may not be the same: the story of God as God is
revealed in this symbol may capture your attention more
easily. You may have heard the symbol knocking, and you
may have opened the door to your hearts. Imagine if you
took the time to do this over the course of several evenings
and prayed with many of the liturgical symbols and actions,
inviting them to dialogue with you and tell you their story.
Your celebrations would come alive; passion would stir in
your hearts and transform your worship!

This process of praying with our symbols counteracts
some of the effects of our cultural emphasis on rational,
linear, discursive *modi operandi* and moves us to a more
balanced, integrated way of being. It is a highly experiential
method. It is extra-liturgical (it uses the symbols of liturgy
but does not occur within a regular liturgy). One advantage
of this type of prayer is that it gives us the time to experience symbols and symbolic action in a leisurely fashion. It
gives us the freedom to linger with them as friends linger

over coffee and dessert. Often, the most meaningful, intimate part of the conversation comes during those moments. This process of prayer calls the celebrants of liturgy more deeply into their own experience.[29] After all, "by experience, we learn from experience."[30] Through praying with symbols, we will be inexplicably drawn to question, renew and deepen the commitment toward which these symbols beckon; we will discover anew the passion and life that has been missing in our worship!

---

[29] The celebrants are *all* those who gather together in the worship space to pray liturgy. Far too often, we still get stuck in the celebrant = priest equation.

[30] Power, "Liturgical Praxis: A New Consciousness at the Eye of Worship," *Worship* 4 (July 1987): 301.

CHAPTER 6

What Part Does Personal Maturity Play?

> Let us profess the truth in love and grow
> to the full maturity of Christ the head.
> Through him the whole body grows,
> and with the proper functioning of the members
> joined firmly together by each supporting ligament,
> builds itself up in love — Ephesians 4:15-16

What significance does a study of personal maturity have for liturgy? To answer this question, let us begin with this passage from Ephesians, which touches on four aspects of personal maturity and growth:

◊ moral

◊ social

◊ psychological

◊ spiritual

When we look at what it means to "profess the truth," we are looking at issues that concern our moral development. To profess the truth is to consciously choose the truth as something that has value for us. If it were not valuable to us, we would choose to profess something else. To profess the truth "in love" indicates not only that we have made a choice about what is valuable, but also that we have a desire to communicate that choice through a relationship based upon deep feeling. This touches our affective, psychosocial development: how we feel, how we relate to ourselves and to those around us, how we respond to the task at hand. To "profess the truth in love" is possible only once we have reached a certain point in our journey toward greater maturity.

We need to have some sense of what we mean by maturity in order to fully comprehend Paul's vision that we grow to "the full maturity of Christ the head." The maturation process goes beyond aging and ripe fruit. Joann Wolski Conn speaks of spiritual maturity as "deep and inclusive love." Does this sound familiar? This book began by stating that liturgy is about loving and being loved. Ms. Conn continues her definition of spiritual maturity by stating that,

> it is the loving relationship to God and others born
> of the struggle to discern where and how God is
> present in the community, in ministry, in suffering,
> in religious and political dissension and in one's
> own "sinfulness."[1]

Liturgy celebrates that loving relationship. It reveals God's presence in re-living and re-membering Jesus' ministry and suffering and the many challenges he made to the times in which he lived. Liturgy assists the process of maturing by asking us to look at our sinfulness in the presence of God's endless mercy: *Kyrie Eleison, Christi Eleison, Kyrie Eleison!*

Liturgy invites us to grow toward "proper functioning" and become "joined firmly together." We must ask ourselves if it is possible to support this process of growth

[1] Joann Wolski Conn, *Spirituality and Personal Maturity*, 14.

toward union and to respond to this invitation liturgy extends to us. If so, how? I believe it is made possible by arriving at an understanding of how we grow and mature. This is precisely what developmental theory articulates.

Defining Developmental Theory

Before we go further, it might help to clarify in basic terms what developmental theory is. Many have looked at the process of human maturation and noticed that there are identifiable phases within this process that have definite characteristics.[2] We "progress" through these phases as we grow and develop. We grow and develop in obvious ways: physically, mentally, socially, morally, psychologically and in the ways we interpret our faith. Psychologists, social scientists and theologians have developed their own systems to describe these phases.

In my opinion, no "system" stands on its own. If we turn to the image of the prism, the whole of the human being is the prism in this instance. When we turn ourselves toward the light, different colors will predominate, depending upon the angle. Each theory picks up and describes a different color or strand of our humanity. Taken as a whole, the process of development and conversion is about the changes we experience in the complex process of living and loving. In part, these changes arise from and return to

---

[2] I prefer to use the words "phase" and "place" rather than "stage" for several reasons. "Phase" lends itself more to the idea of process than to something one completes and puts on the shelf. "Place" blends more with the concept of journey and where one is at a given time during that journey. "Stage," however, feels more acquisition/ achievement-oriented and hierarchical. These are three actions that tenaciously hook us in the twentieth century: acquire, achieve, and order things from highest and best to lowest and worst. We do this automatically, without any awareness of the effects this mindset has on us and on our relationships.

our liturgies. It is easy to understand why Peter Fink notes
that "the goal of all sacramental activity is the development
of a mature Christian person; sacraments are *formative*."[3]
Keeping this in mind, we can draw the following conclusion: Liturgy and development are intimately linked to each
other. "Through the liturgy we share in what was accomplished for our salvation, we are remade and *made new*
through the paschal mystery of Christ."[4] Developmental
theory articulates this process by which we are remade and
made new in Christ.

Developmental Theorists

A cursory survey of the amount of research and writing
being done in the area of human development will verify
that developmental theory is an important concern in many
academic circles today. It is certainly "in vogue." It is also
"in process." Many theorists continue to add to and refine
their own work. One could almost say that there has been
a developmental progression in developmental theory itself. By the early 1980s, the work of many contemporary
theorists had been widely acknowledged and accepted. I
have chosen the following for our examination of personal
development and liturgy:

◊ **Jean Piaget — Cognitive Development:**
Piaget, a Swiss psychologist, addressed the
question of how we know and perceive
things and ideas. He worked within a
framework that drew on biology, scientific
method and the critical philosophy of
Immanuel Kant (1724-1894).

---

[3] Fink, "Sacramental Theology after Vatican II," *New Dictionary of
Sacramental Worship*, 1110; Fink's emphasis. We will look at how
sacraments are transformative later in this chapter.

[4] Irwin, *Liturgy, Prayer and Spirituality*, 132; my emphasis.

◊ **Lawrence Kohlberg — Moral Development:** Kohlberg addresses the question of how we make our choices and why. He has built upon the theories of Piaget.

◊ **Erik Erikson — Psychosocial Development:** Erikson, a German-born psychoanalyst, addressed the question of the tasks that are presented to us at different biological ages and how we master them. He has built upon the work of Sigmund Freud (1856-1939) and links his theory directly to the universal stages of physical maturation.

◊ **James Fowler — Faith Development:** Fowler addresses the question of how we perceive God and our stories of faith at each particular phase of development and how these perceptions affect the choices we make. He acknowledges that he has been influenced by Erikson's eight-stage, psychosocial, epigenetic[5] theory (he refers to it as his interpretive mindset).[6] Although he acknowledges Erikson, he also recognizes that his work fits within the structural framework of Piaget and Kohlberg.

◊ **Robert Kegan — Ego Development:** Kegan addresses the question of how we perceive ourselves and how these perceptions affect the way we form and maintain our relationships. His work is also

---

[5] For a discussion of the differences between epigenetic and hierarchical relationships in the stages, see Walter Conn, *Christian Conversion,* 71-77. Erik Erikson also discusses epigenesis in *Childhood and Society,* 269-273.

[6] Fowler, *Stages of Faith,* 110.

primarily structural and he has been called a
neo-Piagetian. [7]

An Holistic Theory:
The Theory of Conversion

All of the above theories are valuable; each has something
significant to contribute to our understanding of the human
being in process. Many in the field have spent much time
and effort analyzing each theory and proposing which part
of our development comes first. This exercise is somewhat
akin to discussing the chicken and the egg: a great deal of
discussion, no resolution.

In his book, *Christian Conversion*, Walter Conn draws
upon all of the theories and synthesizes them in a comprehensive theory of conversion.[8] Conversion in this context does not refer to the adoption of an entirely new
religion, as used in the phrase, "I converted from Cath-
olicism to Judaism." It means a radical turning toward God,
a change of course precipitated by varying degrees of crisis.
This is not to denigrate other meanings of conversion, most
notably that it is also a turning away from sin. But so often,
this emphasis on the turning away from sin eclipses, at least
partially, the accompanying turning toward God. One complements and completes the other. Regarding this type of
conversion, keep in mind, too, that it "is not just a momen-
tary, once-and-for-all experience...authentic Christian life
requires continuing conversion."[9]

---

[7] Walter Conn, *Christian Conversion*, 36.

[8] Conn's definitive work is a brilliant synthesis illustrated through an
analysis of Thomas Merton's personal development. He states in his
preface (page 3) that he owes much of his work to Bernard Lonergan,
whose "profound influence will be apparent on every page [of this
volume]."

[9] Walter Conn, *Christian Conversion*, 205.

In his book, Conn thoroughly explains the various developmental theories. As he studied this work, he began to realize that movement from one place to another was not as natural as one might think; something more was involved. He identified this "something more" as conversion. In the process of explaining the theories, he relates conversion and development to each other. In considering their relationship, he states that "conversion and development, then, though clearly distinct realities, are intimately connected." He goes on to note that "at key points—development requires conversion, and conversion always occurs within a developmental process."[10] This is particularly appropriate to our work in liturgical renewal because the underlying thrust of liturgy is conversion, as noted in Chapter 2 and by Kevin Irwin:

> Rite and ceremony [liturgy in this case] come from the context of living the Christian life and *lead to a return to a deeper commitment and conversion to the Lord.*[11]

Relating development to conversion has many ramifications because liturgy continually calls us to deeper and deeper conversion. We need to articulate how our particular place in the developmental continuum affects our response to this call. Regis Duffy remarks that "our gospel service cannot ignore the specificity of our current life stage and its crisis"[12]; Gregory Manly and Anneliese Reinhard observe that "full, conscious, active participation in liturgy is possible for a person of a certain stage of human and faith development only."[13] Walter Conn states that,

---

[10] Ibid., 157.

[11] Irwin, *Liturgy, Prayer and Spirituality*, 285; my emphasis.

[12] Duffy, *Real Presence*, 149.

[13] Manly and Reinhard, *Art of Praying Liturgy*, 126.

> just as the meaning of justice differs
> developmentally, so, too, for example, does the
> meaning of love which stands at the center of the
> Christian story.[14]

What needs to be explored more fully, albeit hypotheti-
cally, is the form, content, and meaning that this gospel
service, participation, and love assume during the various
phases of our lives.

How Can Developmental Theory Help Our Renewal Efforts?

How can studying developmental theory help us as we
search for new ways to rekindle the passion in our liturgies,
as we search for new ways to breathe new life into our
ongoing renewal efforts?

First of all, for people who are trying to deepen their
participation and commitment, any tool that increases their
self-awareness will be helpful as long as it does not deteri-
orate into narcissism and navel-gazing. A careful, thoughtful
study of developmental theory and conversion will provide
the legend for the roadmap that charts our life journey.
How helpful it is to know when the road will be a dirt road,
where we will find mountains and when we will encounter
the desert. Developmental theory is the legend that helps
us to name these places in our journeys: it helps us to see
where we are now and where we are being invited to go.

Second, it will also be helpful for those of us who are
trying to implement changes/modifications in our liturgical
celebrations: a knowledge of these theories will give us a
sense of not only what parts of worship are particularly
significant for different people, but more importantly how
people will react to modification, change and catechesis
and why.

---

[14] Walter Conn, *Christian Conversion,* 208.

Third, as stated in the Introduction, knowledge of our growth and development will increase our appreciation of and reverence toward each other. As we gather intimately at table, our ability to accept others grows as our understanding of all of us expands and stretches toward new horizons. Developmental theory cooperates with liturgy in that it helps to lift the veil that often blinds us to the gospel call and message to love without condition. Ignorance breeds contempt, fear and suspicion; it is *not*, as the familiar saying would lead us to believe, bliss. Understanding breeds acceptance, patience and freedom. Understanding binds us together as Body of Christ.

Because each theory focuses on a different part of the evolving person, all have value, and, when synthesized, they provide a model of holistic development that is a much more accurate representation of the process. Each theory has a similar goal: "focus on the person in transformation."[15] Liturgy is formative, as noted above. It helps to mold and shape us into the people we are, the people so loved by God. But it does not stop there. Liturgy is also transformative. It effects "deep change in the lives of those who participate"[16]–change that transforms them in the sacramental presence of the living God who so loves them. Because developmental theory offers a certain wisdom about conversion and transformation, it can be of great benefit to those of us working in liturgical renewal.

Applying Developmental Theory

To present an in-depth analysis of each theorist here would be impossible. Additionally, the theorists discussed here have been arbitrarily selected; other theorists have

---

[15] Walter Conn, *Christian Conversion,* 71.

[16] Kavanagh, *On Liturgical Theology,* 73.

contributed equally valuable work.[17] The point of this chapter is not to teach the theory but to offer some applications of it. The chart in Appendix A names each phase and describes its major highlights according to the six theorists.[18] It is basic and somewhat superficial, but it should impart the feel of the process with enough depth and clarity so that our work of applying these theories to liturgical renewal can begin in earnest.

A Word of Caution

Before we begin an application of developmental theory to the process of liturgical renewal, we should note that there are limitations and drawbacks to the basic concept of developmental theory. These limitations and drawbacks do not negate the usefulness of the various theories—that would be like throwing the baby out with the bath water. To note limitations is to approach the theories realistically and with a sense of balance: they are not a panacea, but they can illuminate our journey.

First of all, it is dangerous to classify anyone into a particular "stage"; this creates certain expectations of an individual that might become self-fulfilling and self-limiting. There is also danger in the nearly inevitable pronounce-

---

[17] In my attempt to understand the impact of developmental theory upon liturgical participation, I have relied on Walter Conn's theory of autonomy and surrender, which is based on the natural drive of all human beings toward self-transcendence. The theorists whom I have selected are the ones he used to develop his own theory of Christian conversion. Regretfully, I have not incorporated the writings of women in my work to any great extent.

[18] The chart is not unique; many people have constructed charts as tools to teach and compare various theories. Keep in mind that each theorist has devoted at least one entire book to the naming and description of the phases of development as he sees them. Should you need or desire further information on any of the particular theorists, it would be wise to consult their original work.

ment of judgment, be it implicit or stated, that views higher "stages" as better; this creates oppression and aggrandizement. However, knowledge of developmental theory "not only will help each of us in our own faith development, but also make us more sensitive to an understanding of the faith of others."[19]

In his book, *Faith Development and Pastoral Care,* James Fowler develops four cautions regarding the use of these theories.[20] These cautions complement and expand upon the ones I have noted, and they are worthwhile restating here. First these theories should not be used for purposes of nefarious comparison or the devaluing of persons. Second, developmental phases are not phases in soteriology. There is no correlation between developmental phases and salvation, no magic place beyond which you are "saved." Third, as pastoral leaders and counselors, educators and spiritual directors, we should not try to propel or impel persons from one place to another. Finally, we should not make movement from one place to another a direct goal of pastoral care, preaching, or Christian education. Our *only* responsibility is to offer support and challenge where it would be beneficial to the person in question. To do this is to help each person see for him/herself where God is calling to him/her at a particular point in time and to encourage a response to that call. It would be wise for us to take Fowler's cautions to heart.

---

[19] Stokes, *Faith Is a Verb,* 24. Although Stokes is referring more to the specific concept of faith expression, his observation is applicable to the whole of developmental theory, especially when it is presented synthetically and holistically.

[20] Fowler addresses this question in Chapter 5, "The Congregation: Varieties of Presence in Selfhood and Faith," pages 79-98, particularly pages 79-81.

The Aspiration of the Faith Community

Having acknowledged that we must be careful in our application of developmental theory, we will first look at the faith community as a whole in terms of its development. The people who make up any group are in many different places in the developmental continuum. No two snowflakes are exactly the same. But the group that is formed by all these different individuals also has a place on that continuum. All the individual snowflakes come together to form a single blanket of snow. Where is the faith community as a whole in its developmental process? The group as a whole has a dream and a vision. James Fowler calls the community's dream or vision its "stage level of aspiration."[21] His is an important concept to consider.

The aspirations of the community provide the individual members with vital energy and hope to guide them forward. Fowler believes that "the stage level of aspiration for a public church...is *Conjunctive Faith*."[22] If we look at how the developmental theorists describe this phase of development, we see that:

◊ It is about caring for others in the broadest and most inclusive of senses because it involves a vision of and for future generations.

◊ It is about choosing to value the dignity of all human beings even above our own self-interest and happiness.

◊ It is about a sense of knowing that there is a "more" but not being clear about the "more."

---

[21] Fowler, *Faith Development and Pastoral Care*, 97.

[22] Ibid., 97.

◊ It is also about inner authority—the value that we choose is chosen because it is the right value, not because someone or something else tells us that it is the right thing to do.

When we place this phase of the developmental continuum in a Christian context, we add a dimension that is at once demanding and frightening, exciting and liberating. It is a dimension that is, above all, passionate. For it is care that is the care of Christ. It is choice that is the choice of Christ. It is knowing that is the knowing of Christ. It is the emergence of an inner authority that becomes more and more the voice of Christ incarnate within us. In this intimate imitation of Christ, we come closer and closer to knowing[23] that "whoever would save his life will lose it, but whoever loses his life for my sake will find it" (Mt 16:25). It is "truly right and just" for our public church to aspire to this place in the developmental process.

Liturgy and the Developmental Process

Just as we can place our community on the developmental continuum, so can we do the same with our liturgy. The developmental phase described above is the *aspiration* of our public church; it is the *reality* of our liturgy. It has been said that the overall liturgy itself is at a developmental "stage" of five based on Fowler's system, four based on Conn's, six based on Kohlberg's, seven based on Erikson's, and five based on Kegan's. (Add them altogether and you arrive at Stage 27; thankfully, Piaget doesn't use numbers or we might need a calculator.) Unlike the community,

---

[23] This "knowing" is a knowing of the heart as opposed to an intellectual knowing of the head. Inner knowing comes from a number of things: experience, faith, reflection, contemplation. This is not to say that intellectual knowing is inferior to inner knowing. Both are needed, but intellectual knowing has been the norm in Western culture for many centuries. It is time to restore the balance.

which, in most cases, only aspires to that level, this is the actual level of liturgy. In looking at the aspiration of the faith community on the developmental continuum, I simply used a brief description. In looking at liturgy, I will specify each theorist and the name of each particular phase. Again, referring to Appendix A provides more details about these phases.

Robert Kegan's Interindividual Stage

As stated previously, all of liturgy is about conversion, a conversion that takes place in a mature, loving relationship with God. This relationship requires a self to give to that relationship; in looking at Kegan's theory of Ego Development, this does not happen until the Interindividual Stage. Up until that point, relationships tend to be based on need and fusion, not selfless giving and intimacy. A relationship based on fusion has a certain feel to it that I would call desperation.[24] The degree of desperation depends on the extent of fusion with the other. If we are honest with ourselves, most of us can probably recall an experience of being involved in a relationship based on fusion. Desperation shows up in many different ways, such as needing to know where the other person in the relationship is all the time, needing constant reassurance of the love of the other person, needing control—needing, needing, needing. The least common denominator in this type of relationship is need. The desperation arises out of a person's fear, conscious or not, that, "If this other person should stop loving me even for an instant, I will not know who I am." In this case, the person has no self to give to the relationship because his/her sense of self is so tied to the other.

On the other hand, a loving relationship based on intimacy has a certain feel to it that I would call freedom. We are free to love simply for the sake of love; free to be who

---

[24] Two other words I would use are "expectation" and "guilt," although there is not space here to draw these out more fully.

we truly are, warts and all; free from the worry of what the other thinks of us because we will not fall apart if they do not like what we are wearing, saying or doing—free, free, free. The least common denominator in a relationship based on intimacy is freedom. A wise spiritual director once told me that when our spiritual journeys are on the right track, they move us always toward greater and greater freedom. We are secure with who we are, and we are ready and willing to surrender ourselves freely to the act of loving God and each other. This is what it means to be in the place that Robert Kegan calls the Interindividual Stage of development. This is the place to which liturgy calls us and the gift it offers to us each and every time we gather to hear the word and break bread together.

Lawrence Kohlberg's Universal Ethical Principles

In order for liturgy to become a true liberator in the fullest sense of the word, it must incorporate ethical values that are universal and not tied to one particular social system. Shifting our values from the particular to the universal is important. When this shift happens, Lawrence Kohlberg says that we have moved into the realm of Universal Ethical Principles. If liturgy were to uncritically embrace the values of one particular group or social system, it would perpetuate whatever oppression and injustice exists in that system.[25] Instead, liturgy adopts basic principles by which we all are to live our lives. These values override any social system—they are "the reciprocity and equality of human rights and of respect for the dignity of human beings as individual persons."[26] Liturgy proclaims gospel values and transforms us so that we may be true to those values, the values of Christ.

---

[25] This has important ramifications for our own Church as it exists as a social system and a purveyor of value.

[26] Walter Conn, *Christian Conversion*, 61.

We can look over and over again at Jesus' persistent challenge to the existing social system of his time. In one instance in Matthew's gospel, Jesus, in typical parabolic form, warns the disciples about the "leaven" of the Pharisees and Sadducees. In equally typical form, they miss his subtle point and begin to worry about not having any bread to eat. Jesus finally spells it out to them:

> "How do you not comprehend that I was not speaking about bread? Beware of the leaven of the Pharisees and Sadducees." Then they understood that he was not telling them to beware of leaven of bread, but of the teaching of the Pharisees and Sadducees (Mt 16:11-12).

Thus, the gospel calls us to begin to examine our values and where they come from, to be critical about what we choose. The gospel asks that we separate ourselves from the prevailing social order. Liturgy demands a liberation from unexamined, taken-for-granted values—a liberation that poses a serious challenge to existing systems. Tom Driver believes that the predominant function of any ritual celebration is to bring about some change in the existing order.

In the context of our Christian faith, this means ongoing, deeper conversion and transformation. This does not happen without an unwelcome upset to our familiar apple cart. Jesus was not hung on a cross because he endeared himself to the local authorities and religious leaders. As Driver says so well, "a rite that has lost its power to transform [not only us but our social/political systems as well] runs a strong risk of becoming mere show."[27] When we are able to act on what is manifestly fair rather than what serves our own self-interest (be it the interest of an individual or a particular group), we are honoring what our liturgy seeks from us; we are operating within Kohlberg's Universal Ethical Principles.

[27] Driver, *Magic of Ritual*, 95.

Walter Conn's Critical Moral Conversion

Each individual committed to fostering freedom and justice must adopt those values as his/her own and not because a specific group has deemed those values the most worthwhile. The individual must freely choose for him/herself, unencumbered by any "shoulds" or other external coercion. This requires Conn's Critical Moral (Cognitive) Conversion, and it complements Kohlberg's Universal Ethical Principles as well as Kegan's Interindividual Stage of Ego Development. As Conn himself says so beautifully, "One must be one's own tailor, regardless of the brilliance of one's favorite designer."[28] One cannot be one's own tailor if one does not have an established sense of self any more than one can give a self freely in love if one does not have a separate self.

Liturgy's commitment to freedom and justice, which arises from God's deep love for us, transcends every culture's values and choices.

James Fowler's Conjunctive Stage

Any commitment to liberation must obviously be fed by a vision of that which has not yet been realized. This vision does not appear until Fowler's Conjunctive Stage. This "stage" produces much tension. At this "stage," the person sees the status quo and and also sees how much better things could be. The "seer," as the person in this phase of development is called, must balance the two.

Liturgy greets and welcomes us where we are right now and, at the same time, constantly draws us into its vision. Liturgy's vision of God's encompassing love for us ("for God so loved the world") challenges us to bring peace and justice into a world overwhelmed daily by war and violations of human rights. Tension is bound to arise.

---

[28] Walter Conn, *Christian Conversion*, 127.

Erik Erikson's Intimacy and Generativity

Action must be based on what is right in and of itself; it must not be based on individual need fulfillment. We see this emerging in Kohlberg's and Conn's descriptions. Again, this action will flow out of a psychosocial development that has embraced Intimacy and Generativity, Erikson's sixth and seventh tasks that yield love and care. The ability to enter into relationships with a well-developed sense of self and to enter them freely as Kegan describes is complemented by Erikson's observation that, at this place, a person will "develop the ethical strength to abide by such commitments, even though they may call for significant sacrifices and compromises."[29]

Our liturgy is often referred to as "the sacrifice of the Mass" because it celebrates the result of Christ's strong commitment to God and to us: the cross. In Eucharistic Prayer I, we recall the many saints who had the strength to die for their commitment to their faith. In the Concluding Rite, we are sent forth to love and serve in the same way.

Liturgical Prayer and the Developmental Process

In the simple opening prayer taken from the Tenth Sunday in Ordinary Time, we can see some of the dynamics of developmental theory at work during our celebration of liturgy:

> Father in heaven,
> words cannot measure the boundaries of love
> for those born to new life in Christ Jesus.
> Raise us beyond the limits this world imposes,
> so that we may be free to love as Christ teaches
> and find our joy in your glory.

This prayer expresses our recognition that we have moved beyond—surrendered and transcended—our own

---

[29] Erikson, *Childhood and Society*, 262.

little life and we have been born to "new life in Christ." We pray that we be lifted beyond any social system—"raise us beyond the limits this world imposes"—so that we may be "free" to love as Christ has taught us. The value we choose is the value of love; we ask "to love as Christ teaches." We pray to love in the way that God loves us through Christ. The spirit in which we choose to live out that love is the spirit of freedom. We appropriate this value of love by ourselves, independent of what someone else might dictate our primary value to be. We appropriate this value, not for our own benefit and gain, but simply to glorify God: may we "find our joy in your glory."

This simple prayer illuminates the place on the developmental continuum toward which liturgy guides our faith community.

◊ Words can no longer measure the
boundaries of love; we become visionaries
(Fowler's Conjunctive Stage).

◊ In the freedom to love, we have transcended
the immediate world and the small self
(Kegan's Interindividual Ego).

◊ We pray to be freed from the world's limits
so that we may make our own choices
(Conn's Cognitive Conversion).

◊ We choose to extend the love and care of
Christ (Erikson's Generativity).

◊ Our joy does not depend any longer on what
feels good or what fills our own immediate
need (Kohlberg's Universal Ethical
Principles). It rests in the glory of God.

This is liturgy's vision, its prophetic call. Though many celebrants gathered as assembly may not reach this place in their developmental journey, their worship experience is no less valid, prayerful, or authentic. Liturgy stands as the promise of what is yet to be, of the light that beckons us forth. The profoundness of the promise and the brightness of the light reach out to all of us, independent of where we are developmentally. Liturgy humbly serves to guide us in the right direction, encourage us when we stumble, and challenge us when we grow complacent.

Individuals and the Developmental Process

We have looked at how community aspires to a particular place in the developmental continuum; we have looked at our liturgy as being in that place. Now we will look at the impact of individual development on particular aspects of liturgical celebration. Our personal images of God shape the way we relate to that God in our worship: "The way we conceive of God has everything to do with the way we conceive of ourselves in relationship to God and to one another in the community of faith."[30] Our ability to communicate through symbols impacts the way we participate. Our ability to participate impacts how deeply the gospel message moves us to become loving servants and Body of Christ. Each of these aspects is intimately connected to the others; a change in any one will precipitate a change in all the others.

Where we as individuals are developmentally affects every aspect of our liturgical prayer. And our liturgical prayer will affect where we are developmentally. As Peter Fink has succinctly noted: "Each of the things that we do in liturgical assembly...has the power to tug at our behavior, our values, and our working images of life, of people, of God, of ourselves."[31] This is significant in our understanding of liturgy—not only does our own development

---

[30] Hughes, "Liturgy and Justice: Bridging the Gap," *Modern Liturgy* 18, no. 8: 10.

[31] Fink, *Worship: Praying the Sacraments*, 145.

bear on liturgy, but the symbols/images and actions of liturgy bear on us.

A short story might serve to illustrate how our personal development and liturgy are intimately connected and work hand in hand.

> A second-grade teacher is about to enter his
> classroom and begin the school day. From the
> moment he had gotten up until the moment he
> arrived at school, everything that could
> possibly have gone wrong in his life had: the
> hot water tank had developed a leak and there
> was no hot water for a shower; the dog had
> thrown up on the new dining room rug; his left
> front tire had gone flat overnight. Now he is
> running late, which compounds the problem.
> It is one of those mornings. And of all days for
> this to happen. He and his class have planned a
> special puppet show; they are expecting many
> parents to come at 10 A.M. for the command
> performance. His class is full of enthusiasm and
> smiles when he finally storms through the
> door. At this critical moment, one of two
> things can happen. Either his bad mood will
> dampen the class' spirits and the performance,
> or the smiles and enthusiasm of the children
> will transform him.

Liturgy and our personal development are like that. Sometimes, our individual development will affect liturgy and we will simply not be able to "be there" to the degree that we might like. And sometimes, liturgy will move us so deeply that we are transformed, moved beyond the place where we were when we began to worship. Many of us have experienced this; sometimes the movement is dramatic, but more often the transformation is gentle and it happens "bit by bit."

To illustrate the effect of personal development on liturgy and liturgy's potential to transform us, we will draw sketches of three adults who are at different places on the development continuum. Each sketch will address the aspects mentioned above:

◊ the person's perception/image/concept of God

◊ the person's experience of relationship to God and to the gathered assembly

◊ the person's ability to communicate through the symbolic language of liturgy

◊ the person's willingness and ability to participate fully, consciously and actively

◊ the person's depth of commitment to love and serve God and, thus, as God is present and incarnate in all of us, to love and serve each other

The three people in the following sketches are in different places on the development continuum. Keep in mind that development and conversion are fluid processes, and the various "stages" are not tidy boxes in which to confine and restrict people. People move forward and backward between "stages" depending on a complex set of factors, including socio-economic status, genetic makeup, family experience, and life environment, to name a few.

Helen

We introduce Helen as our first example. To a great degree, Helen would identify herself with the following "stages":

◊ Erikson's Identity/Confusion

◊ Kohlberg's Interpersonal Concordance

◊ Fowler's Synthetic/Conventional

◊ Kegan's Interpersonal

◊ Conn's Uncritical Moral

Helen is in her mid-forties. She has been married for twenty-five years, has two children in college and one in middle school. For her, God is very much the authoritative figure who helps her to make decisions in her everyday life. Jesus figures in her prayer as a friend. Most of the time she feels that if she tries to do the right thing by God, God will do the right thing by her. A few minor crises in her life have made her wonder about that, but she feels fairly comfortable with her perception of things.

Helen goes to church faithfully every Sunday and makes all the first Fridays. She enjoys going to church; it is a pleasant experience for her most of the time, partly because it affords her the opportunity to see her friends and socialize with them at the coffee hour afterward. Her participation at Mass varies from perfunctory to prayerful and sometimes moving. She doesn't reflect about it much; no one has ever invited her to do so and the thought has seldom occurred to her. She is fairly satisfied with the way things are at her church. She was a bit unhappy with the electric keyboard and all those trumpets on the Feast of Christ the King and she did tell the pastor that she missed the banners during the Lent that the Liturgy Committee went for the austere, ascetic look. She would like to see if everyone could hold hands during the Our Father—they always did that in her church in Boseville—and one of these weeks she might just mention it to the Liturgy Committee Chairperson.

Helen makes choices based on what the people she respects have told her is good and right to do—her friends, her husband, her mother. She often finds herself wondering if the choice she has just made will be OK with the people she cares about. Sometimes, she has a deep longing to just say the heck with it and make a choice that she didn't have to worry about. It can be very tiring to wonder about what everyone else thinks, but it has become such a habit.

She belongs to the Outreach Committee. She joined the committee because several of her friends had asked her to. She saw this as an opportunity to deepen her friendships and do a little something for the church.

José

We introduce José as our second example. To a great degree, José would identify himself with the following "stages":

◊ Erikson's Identity/Confusion

◊ Kohlberg's Authority/Social Order

◊ Fowler's Individual/Reflective

◊ Kegan's Institutional

◊ Conn's Affective

José is a reservations clerk in his late twenties. He is engaged. He goes to school at night to be a computer analyst. He prides himself on his work for the airline and he has done pretty well in school. His parents initially did not like his fiancée, and there was a great deal of argument and hard feelings for a long time over this. José began to look differently at the way things were after that; he now has his own apartment, sees his parents occasionally and feels fairly secure and independent. God is somewhat of an enigma to him; because José has begun to think many things out for himself, God is no longer the supreme authority he once was. The relationship is an uneasy one, one of those, "You can be here, God, but let me do my own thing and don't interfere too much." True intimacy is not possible because José is concerned with being in charge, although friendship and love are important to him.

José goes to church sporadically. He enjoys talking to the pastor about what is going on in the church-at-large. He went to a couple of adult education programs that the Education Committee sponsored and he thought that they were fairly interesting. They helped him figure out some of the questions he had been struggling with. He has begun to look at all the values and symbols he had always taken for granted and to weed out what doesn't make sense to him anymore. Last year, the church sponsored a program called "Rejuvenate Our Symbols." He never did see the point to it—what difference did it make if they used a lot of water or a little? Or if they used bread that was real loaves or the little wafers they had been using forever? Or if they did get a big fancy book for the gospels? These things just don't grab him much. When he does go to church, he is pretty aware of everything that is going on, but he keeps his distance, always weighing and evaluating, staying on top of things. Sometimes, he would like to relax a little and just let things be, but that's pretty scary, too.

José considers himself fairly committed to good causes; he makes his choices based on what is right. He determines what is right for him by the rules and the laws that keep things in order and running smoothly. Even though he finds himself asking many questions, things are more or less black and white—what is right is right and what is wrong is wrong. He genuinely does care for other people; his own family was near poverty for many years and he has been very dedicated at working for the Food Bank that is run by the Council of Churches in his town. It is the right thing to do.

Evelyn

We introduce Evelyn as our third example. To a great degree, Evelyn would identify herself with the following "stages":

◊ Erikson's Generation/Stagnation

◊ Kohlberg's Universal Ethical Principles

◊ Fowler's Conjunctive

◊ Kegan's Interindividual

◊ Conn's Cognitive

Evelyn is a widow in her early fifties. She has two children, one who is gay and one who is married with one child. Evelyn dotes on her granddaughter, born a year and a half after her husband died of cancer. Katie has been a gift from God, the light that helped her to move out of a darkness that had threatened to devour her. After her husband died, nothing made sense. God was her adversary for a long time, her punisher. It took her a long time to sort out her feelings. It was an experience at Eucharist one Sunday shortly after Easter that made her realize that God was in the midst of her grief, a loving presence who was crying with her, not an enemy trying to punish her.

Evelyn experienced a radical coming home to God through her experience of that Eucharist. Symbols have become alive and very moving to her once again; they draw her deeper into the mystery to which she can't quite put words. She feels connected to each and every person in the assembly—almost as though there were an invisible web that has woven them all together. She sees a great deal of injustice not only in the world, but in her own church. She is often caught between understanding where people are coming from (or at least having a willingness to listen to their point of view) and seeing a need to change things so that all people's rights can be respected.

Evelyn serves on the liturgy committee and is fairly open to hearing new ideas. She is deeply invested in living a Christian life, but seeks to know about other faiths as well. One of her closest friendships is with a woman who is Hindu. Their discussions on religion have been fascinating and stimulating to her. She has been more and more aware lately of meeting Jesus in the strangest of experiences—

even in the chance encounter in the grocery store when she greets the stooped old woman passing by. There is a sensitivity and a connectedness to all strangers that continues to grow. The words of the gospel seem to take on added meaning every time she hears them.

The Helens, Josés, and Evelyns are a part of every liturgical celebration. They are each a part of us in some way, whether we recognize it or not. They represent, in a general way, either where we are right now, where we have been or where we might be. Each one brings a gift to the assembly, but it is important to recognize that there is an underlying tension and source of "unfreedom" in all of their lives. They will be set free only as they experience God's unconditional love more deeply; with deep and compassionate concern, God describes that love:

> Because you are precious in my eyes and glorious,
> and because I love you,
> I give men in return for you
> and peoples in exchange for your life.
> Fear not, for I am with you;
> from the east I will bring back your descendants,
> from the west I will gather you (Is 43:4-5).

Liturgy reveals God's love in myriad ways. Remember, God does not need liturgy; we do. We may hear God's love through the words of the gospel; we may see, taste or touch God's love through a particular symbol; we may feel God's love as a vague gnawing or a steady warmth in the innermost depths of our hearts.

For the Helens of the assembly, God's unconditional love will help them to move beyond the tenuous, unstable place of defining who they are by the relationships they have. For the Josés of the assembly, God's unconditional love will help them move beyond the exhausting, lonely place of defending who they are by how well they are able to organize and control their relationships and roles into a system of self. For the Evelyns of the assembly, God's unconditional love will help them move beyond the often confusing, challenging place of seeing the both/and in all situations.

We can help the Helens in the assembly by inviting them to be more reflective about their worship—full, conscious and active participation is not a reality for most of them, but inviting them to be critical about what they are doing could be the opening they need. One opening, one deep, unsettling experience during liturgy might turn their tidy world upside down. It might allow them to see that they do not have to cling to relationships or the love of others in order to define who they are. An authentic experience of God's love as lived out in liturgy will give them what they need to move from this tenuous place and begin to see themselves in a new light.

We can help the Josés in the assembly by providing them with a safe place to be, a place where they feel accepted, a place where their need for independence and a little breathing room is respected. Once relaxed and comfortable, they may become more open to experience God's unconditional love, an experience that may help the Josés out there realize that they are far more than their roles, duties and institutions have lead them to believe. Once their eyes are opened to a new vision of self, they may become free to embrace others with a deeper sense of true self, free to see that life is not either/or but both/and, free to see a deeper connectedness between all of us.

We can help the Evelyns in the assembly by providing a listening ear that is willing to hear them out as they sift and sort through the many paradoxes that they hold in tension. Through the support and love of the gathered assembly, through the action of word and Eucharist, they may come to be lifted out of the paradox, come to a place where it is no longer the focal point of their prayer, come to a place where they can let it go and rest simply in God. As a short, anonymous prayer poetically describes, "When I have come to rest in thee, Beloved, I have come simply home."

Is it naive to believe that liturgy can effect such change and offer this type of support? If we honestly believe in all that has been said up until this point, then liturgy does have that potential. We must begin to see change and movement from one place to another as a cooperative effort invited by God, sometimes initiated and sometimes supported by our participation in liturgy. It is a journey that is described well by developmental theory. All work together in a flowing process of webs and threads, connections and relationships. At the heart of the process is the "full maturity of Christ" whose deepest desire is that we "might have life and have it to the full" (Jn 10:10).

What is our role in this process? James Fowler sums it up well, remarking that we, as public church and gathered assembly, are called to "work consciously and intentionally to become a nurturing and stimulating ecology of care and vocation, meeting and embracing persons at their various points of development."[32] In doing this, we truly become the human instruments of our God; we truly come to live out the dying, rising Christ in our daily life.

---

[32] Fowler, *Faith Development and Pastoral Care*, 97.

CHAPTER 7

What Part Does Cultural Maturity Play?

For we are to be changed into God and sometime
made One with God, so that what is
God's shall be ours and what is ours, God's:
our hearts and God's are to be one heart;
our body and God's, one body. So, too, it shall be
with our senses, wills, thoughts, faculties,
and members: they are all to be transported into
God, so that we feel with God and are made aware
of God in every part of the body and soul.
— Meister Eckhart[1]

This quotation is taken from one of Eckhart's early works
(c. 1290): *The Talks of Instruction*, no. 20, entitled, "About
the body of our Lord, how often one should partake of it,

---

[1] Blakney, *Meister Eckhart*, 28. For those readers who are unfamiliar
with Eckhart, he was a thirteenth-century German mystic. Some of
his works were condemned by the Catholic Church in 1328, but
within the last several decades, his works have found a large
readership. I have substituted the word "God" for the word "him" for
the sake of inclusive language.

with what devotion and in what manner." This is Eckhart's experience of Eucharist, his articulation of the desire and revelation of God that resides in the very heart of our liturgy. This experience, which stretches far beyond the ability of words to describe it, seems to speak of a profoundly deep experience of conversion. This experience is not a peak or a high, not a private acquisition to place on the shelf like a trophy, but a place of rest and seamless unity into which we have been led through Eucharist. This experience is the heart of mature Christian desire and response.

Assessing Our Culture

I chose to begin this chapter with the quotation from Eckhart because mature Christian desire and response contrast starkly with the desire and response of the American culture. We can illustrate this contrast by rewriting this beautiful, moving passage from the perspective of a modern observer of twentieth-century America. This observer wants to articulate the desire and response of our nation based on his/her experience of watching the nightly news for a week. To experience the full impact, I have placed Eckhart's passage beside it:

For we are to be changed
into God and sometime
made One with God, so that
what is God's shall be ours
and what is ours, God's: our
hearts and God's are to be
one heart; our body and
God's, one body. So, too, it
shall be with our senses,
wills, thoughts, faculties,
and members: they are all to
be transported into God, so
that we feel with God and
are made aware of God in
every part of the body and
soul.

For America is to be
charged with leadership and
sometime made ruler over
all, so that what is the
world's shall be ours and
what is ours shall remain
ours; our hearts are to stand
over, above and separate
from the hearts of other
nations. So, too, it shall be
with natural resources,
material goods, technology,
money, and power: they are
all to be transported into
America, so that we feel
important and powerful in
every part of our cultural
body and soul.

I balked initially at this description of our culture. It
seemed too harsh. But in light of many things, especially
the travesty of the Persian Gulf War,[2] I believe it is an
accurate description. This is not to deny the vision and
work of our many activist and philanthropic organizations
who are trying to counteract the prevailing situation; it is
simply to state what continues to be the overall American
mindset and desire. We can express this somewhat face-
tiously: the person with the most toys wins and whoever
wins is the most powerful.

It might prove informative and provocative to do another
comparison. These selections provocatively contrast the

---

[2] I choose to use the word "travesty" based on the following statistics:
70,000-115,000 troops and 2,500-3,000 civilians died in the war.
100,000-120,000 civilians died after the war due to civil unrest,
starvation, and plague, all of which stemmed from the effects of the
war. 170,000 children under the age of five will die of diarrhea and
malnutrition, again deaths which can be traced to the effects of the
war. These statistics are taken from an article by R. A. Schroth, S.J.,
"Media Mirrors Mixed America after Gulf War," *National Catholic
Reporter* 28, no. 13 (January 31, 1992): 16.

experience of communal life found in Chapter 2 in the Acts of the Apostles with the life we have today in our global community. Carl Sagan's piece is taken from a secular parable that was told at the Global Forum of Spiritual and Parliamentary Leaders, which took place in Moscow in January 1990. His thought-provoking article, "Avert a Common Danger," appeared in *Parade Magazine* on March 2, 1992.

They devoted themselves to the apostles' instruction and the communal life, to the breaking of bread and the prayers...Those who believed shared all things in common; they would sell their property and goods, dividing everything on the basis of each one's need. They went to the temple area together every day, while in their homes they broke bread. With exultant and sincere hearts they took their meal in common, praising God and winning the approval of all people (Acts 2:42, 44-47).

Imagine humanity as a village of 100 families. Sixty-five families in our village are illiterate; 90 do not speak English; 70 have no drinking water at home; 80 have no members who have ever flown in an airplane. Seven families own 60 percent of the land and consume 80 percent of all the available energy. They have all the luxuries. Sixty families are crowded onto 10 percent of the land. Only one family has a university education.

We cannot be blind to the place and the responsibility the American nation as a whole has in those statistics. And while the passage from Acts (the first of three that describe what the early Christian community was like) is obviously written in ideal terms,[3] it is, nonetheless, intimately tied to the community's experience of Jesus and to its eucharistic celebrations. "In their homes they broke bread." Their real experience of Christ moved them to study and live commu-

---

[3] We know from a careful study of Paul's letters that the Christian communities fell short of that ideal time and time again.

nally. Their real experience of breaking bread-become-body of Christ moved them to reach out to others in the same way that Jesus had. The more they reached out, the more they discovered the risen Christ within their midst. The more they discovered this Christ in their midst, the more they prayed together. It became an endless cycle of deeper and deeper conversion into the life, death and resurrection of Christ, into his passion and love for God and others. This conversion does not come about without its own particular pain and struggle. We need only to think of Ananias and his wife.[4]

Our twentieth-century culture is far removed from the picture that Luke portrays in Acts. Not only is it not our experience, *it is not even our ideal.* I do not think that the effect of this disparity on worship can be overestimated. The basic white, middle-class American values of consumerism and materialism, affluence, media, competition, individualism, instant gratification, narcissism, self-preoccupation, and promotion[5] have been adopted by all classes of people as the optimal values for the society-at-large. Mary Collins notes that all cultural systems will bring out their dominant symbols and their cherished values in their most elaborate public rituals. "The interplay of symbols of youth, sex, money, physical force, male dominance, and consumer goods in the ritual of the televised Super Bowl constitutes the central cultural performance of the United States at the end of the twentieth century."[6]

---

[4] The story of Ananias and his wife, which appears in Acts 5, is one of a couple who fell dead upon realizing that their scheme and lie had been a scheme and lie not only to the community but to God.

[5] In his introduction to *Inviting the Mystic, Supporting the Prophet* by L. Patrick Carroll and Katherine Dyckman, Peter J. Henriot does a commendable job discussing the American condition as well as the issue of commitment to follow Jesus in the work of the Reign.

[6] Collins, *Worship: Renewal to Practice*, 101.

Culture and Liturgy

It is not difficult to see that the values expressed by the symbols Mary Collins mentions are, for the most part, in direct opposition to our Christian ritual and gospel values. The meeting of these two value systems can be likened to the collision of a large mass of warm air with one of cold in the upper atmosphere, producing violent thunderstorms. Perhaps every church bulletin board should post what appear to be more or less permanent weather conditions: "Violent storm expected during liturgy today; bring umbrellas and galoshes."

Many have judged the culture as a whole and added a few comments about Americans as individuals as well. Things do not look good for the defendants. It might be interesting to note what some of the jurors have said about the effect of culture on liturgy as they returned their verdict of "guilty as charged":

> Both our commercial, technological culture and our intellectual, rationalist tradition militate against this kind of awakening to things and to the symbolic function of things, of which a genuine liturgical renewal stands so desperately in need.
> — Robert Hovda

> A culture which is oriented to efficiency and production has made us insensitive to the symbolic function of persons and things. Also, the same cultural emphasis on individuality and competition has made it more difficult for us to appreciate the liturgy as a *personal-communal* experience.
> — Environment and Art in Catholic Worship
> (emphasis in original)

> This excessive individuality, this cultural egoism, this vain self-regard, this communal over-preoccupation with self, this societal self-conceit has made a difference for liturgy.
> — James Empereur

The sovereign individual is freed as society is bent
to his service. One asks not what one can do for the
common good, but what the common good, the
oppressor par excellence, can do for me.

— Aidan Kavanagh

Forgiveness requires awareness of human
vulnerability, requires compassion, requires a
readiness to admit we're all in this together. Our
public cultural style generally denies this, telling us
it's every man for himself. So self-actualization is
valued and pursued as achievable without self
denial; competitiveness is pitted against
cooperation; aggressiveness is praised and human
weakness masked by posturing.

— Mary Collins

Our culture knows little of how to prepare us for
the attentive waiting of the neutral zone.

— James Fowler

When we put these pieces together, the completed picture is not an encouraging one for our liturgical celebrations. We are living in a culture whose approach to life has
made it difficult to communicate through symbols. Our
growing scientific ability to dissect and expose everything
and our technological ability to fix just about anything has
broken apart our symbols. We have been left with neither
the patience nor the sensitivity for the delicate workings of
the symbolic structure, for the awakening to things that is
the promise of their process. We are also living in a culture
whose love affair with romantic, pioneer-type individualism and pull-yourself-up-by-your-bootstraps competition
has left the desire for communal life withering on the vine.
How do we surrender to the call to become Body of Christ
when we are busy defending our own personal territory
and looking out for our own interests? And finally, we are
living in a culture which is moving at such a rapid pace,
whose every space is so filled with things and the noises of
things that we honestly do not know how to wait, let alone

how to "wait in joyful hope." We have no space or time for silence, for reverence, for contemplation, for imagination to grow and to nourish our liturgies.

Culture and Developmental Theory

Is it possible to apply developmental theory to our culture? Our culture is as much an entity as our community and our liturgy. It has definite values. It also goes through some process by which those values are chosen. Our culture, through its government, forms relationships with other groups and countries. As a culture, we have a sense of self, however immature, limited and constrained it might be. This is why the loss of the Vietnam War was so difficult for so many—it threatened the nation's image as a winner, as all-good and all-powerful. America is not a loser, and it has no patience for them. This is why the Persian Gulf War proved so attractive for many. It restored the old image. Developmental theory addresses all these areas: values, the way we choose values, relationships, self-image. Developmental theory has a great deal to teach us in these areas.

The American culture, taken as a whole and brightly displayed through its influential, mesmerizing modes of advertising,[7] is probably at Conn's stage of Premoral Conversion: it is radically egocentric and values whatever it finds satisfying.

Our culture does not go beyond Piaget's Concrete Operational thinking. We may possess some ability to reflect critically on how our consumerism and materialism affects the overall global environment and economy, but we have no desire to act on or respond to that reflection. We can

---

[7] Keep in mind that, in this culture, the media is extremely influential not only in promoting values but as an indicator of those values; to ascertain what is of value to a culture, one can begin with a subject survey of its media.

construct models of the future that are realistic extrapola-
tions based on current conditions, but again we see no
desire to use those constructions as a basis for action.

Our culture finds itself capable of using and developing
new technology; it has thus achieved Erikson's vision of
Industry/Competence, but it seems stuck there. It does not
know itself other than through its needs for more (Kegan's
Imperial Self): it manipulates whole groups of people to
satisfy those needs. Never was this more apparent than
during the Persian Gulf War. It enthusiastically embraces
causes so that it can feel good about itself, then it casts them
aside.[8] Morally, it embraces a fair exchange methodology
(Kohlberg's Instrumental Relativist): "You do this for me,
I'll do this for you."

This is not a vision of hope nor is it a vision of maturity,
but I do believe it is a vision of reality. There are bright spots
here and there (for example, concerned environmental
groups), but the overall cultural drive is a powerful one that
stands in direct opposition to the call of the gospel. When
we approach liturgy and liturgical renewal, we need to be
aware of the stumbling blocks erected by this culture.
While we cannot take on an entire culture, neither do we
need to throw up our hands in a gesture of despair. We can
begin to intentionally reject these cultural values quietly,
firmly, non-violently, and embrace the values of loving
service and self-surrender. We can begin to live the gospel.
We can open ourselves to the Word and willingly "undergo

---

[8] In an interesting article on Earth Day, "Will the Ballyhoo Go Bust?" by
Eugene Linden, *Time Magazine* (April 23, 1990): 86, the author
comments that "it is possible that the environment might be better
served if consumers had no such outlet [a reference to blowing off
steam on Earth Day] and were forced to do some quiet soul searching
about how their individual choices contribute to the world's environmental problems." How easy it is for us as a worshipping assembly to
give lip service to the often demanding gospel message that "no
servant can serve two masters" (Lk 16:13) and then return to luxuri-
ous homes or dreams and plans for such homes. Our cultural worship
of materialism and consumerism is subtle, pervasive, difficult to resist.

the cleansing and liberating cauterizing of heart and soul that will fit us to be instruments of God's new creation."[9] We can begin to encourage the quiet soul-searching that Eugene Linden advocates[10]; it is, perhaps, the best avenue for transformation and the one used so effectively by Christ.

Our Resistance to Conversion

Faced with the disparity between the first-century Christian community ideals and the realities of the twentieth-century American culture, is it any wonder that our liturgical celebrations are somewhat lacking and perfunctory? Given the overwhelming gap between what could be and what is, is it any wonder that we do not engage in full, conscious and active participation? Walter Conn points out that "No one wants to change a more or less effective *and* comfortable pattern of living...there will, of course, always be some kind of resistance."[11] In the language of children, the Velveteen Rabbit wishes "that he could become [real] without these uncomfortable things happening to him." Indeed, why should we be any different? We must expect some concern, some worry, some anxiety, some resistance to liturgy's call for our ongoing conversion, personally and communally. It is normal.

How many of you can recall being in a conversation with someone as he/she begins to tell you a truth that is too painful for you to hear? You might change the subject; you might stammer and stutter; you might look away; you might invent a reason that you have to leave right away. Sometimes you might even feel sick—a convenient headache or upset stomach. Just as we are endlessly creative in "real life"

---

[9] Fowler, *Faith Development and Pastoral Care*, 51.

[10] See footnote #8 on previous page.

[11] Walter Conn, *Christian Conversion*, 207.

situations when we want to avoid something, we are also creative in our schemes to protect ourselves from the conversion and transformation that is inevitable in our journeys toward God.

Liturgy calls for our conversion, invites us to embrace "what is longing to be" and let go of "what is." It is human nature to balk at this. We will encounter resistance within ourselves individually, and we will encounter resistance within ourselves communally. The difference between what happens in personal and communal prayer is a quantitative difference, not a qualitative one. It simply happens in a larger context. Just as resistance shows itself in personal prayer, I believe it manifests itself as well in our communal prayer. Resistance is positive! It tells us that we are experiencing God's love in some way; we are hearing God's call. Our experience of God's love may be as intense as feeling that we have been "set on fire" (CSL, n. 10); our experience of God's call may be as small as a "tiny whispering sound" (1 Kgs 19:12). Resistance to God's love and call may manifest itself in complaints of boredom during liturgy, inordinate attention to small details, excessive planning, leaving early, sporadic attendance. Anything that takes our attention away from the actual matter at hand—celebrating liturgy with our heart and soul—may be a form of resistance.

Our patterns of resistance have had a detrimental effect on the Vatican II vision of full, conscious and active participation. Resistance in our liturgical celebrations is like throwing a blanket upon the fire. Full, conscious and active participation will come only when we are able to recognize these patterns and begin to break them down. This takes patience and support, reflection and prayer. This patience, support, reflection and prayer need to happen not only one-on-one but also within the context of the full community. In their book, *The Practice of Spiritual Direction*, William Barry and William Connolly devote an entire chapter to the development of relationship and resistance. Even though it is geared toward the one-on-one relationship of a

person with his/her God, it is a simple step to translate and
apply the truths in that chapter to the relationship of a
community with its God.

To begin to look at resistance sensitively and without
judgment is to open the doors to freedom and courage in
relationship. It is easy for most of us to understand and
identify with Jesus' prayer in the garden, "Abba (O Father),
you have the power to do all things. Take this cup away
from me." Freedom from resistance will bring us the courage to pray from our hearts the completion of that prayer,
"But let it be as you would have it, not as I" (Mk 14:36). At
that point we have assented to the Paschal Mystery in the
depth of our being.

Becoming Aware of Resistance in Your Community

How might you begin to recognize and break down
patterns of resistance within your community? You might
set aside some time, either individually or communally, to
begin to look at how resistance during liturgy might manifest itself, why resistance happens, and how you can begin
to recognize it. Keep in mind that resistance is a lifetime
companion for all of us, and there is no "instant" formula
that will make it go away forever.

The following suggestions might work well in your community, although you may not find them easy. Breaking
down patterns of resistance is not something you "accom-
plish" over the course of a single evening (or even a series
of evenings). You may begin the process individually, in a
community, or in a small faith-sharing group. Resistance is
an integral part of being human, and it is also often full of
subtlety and nuance. We never reach a point where resistance is absent, either personally of communally. What you
can hope for, with God's bountiful graces, is a greater
awareness of the patterns. The awareness will make a
difference!

Naming Distractions

Name times when you are distracted or when you notice distraction around you. This is a vital first step. You might begin with the cursory list given earlier:

◊ Complaints of boredom during liturgy

◊ Inordinate attention to small details

◊ General lack of attention

◊ Excessive or elaborate planning for liturgy

◊ Leaving early

◊ Sporadic attendance

Continuing to Notice

Notice these behaviors in yourself and in your community at large. Add to the list as you notice any pattern of behavior that seems to take away from your celebrations or seems impertinent to them. Again, at this point, you are simply noticing these patterns.

Asking Why

Once you have spent time noticing, it is time to ask, "Why?" Why are people bored? Why do they leave early? Why is the liturgy committee so caught up in planning? Why aren't people paying attention? After you have arrived at some initial conclusions, ask yourself if there are any deeper reasons.

Looking at Your Experience of God during Liturgy

Move away from looking at the distracting behaviors that occur during your community's celebrations of liturgy. Begin to look at the movement of God that is happening within you and within the assembly during liturgy. What might be difficult about this experience of God? What do you do when you encounter any difficult experience?

Connecting Resistance to Experience of God

Name the myriad distractions as a form/pattern of resistance. Look at these patterns and your experiences of God at the same time. Then begin to connect your resistance to experiences of and with God that may not be comfortable or easy. Remember the words of the Velveteen Rabbit:

> ...the idea of growing shabby and losing his eyes
> and whiskers was rather sad. He wished that he
> could become [Real] without these uncomfortable
> things happening to him.

Often, the naming of the resistance and the connection to an encounter with God will be all that is needed to begin to break the patterns down.

PART III

TOWARD
GREATER
WHOLENESS

CHAPTER 8

Where Do We Go from Here?

Ritual catechesis does not have as its task the
identification of a single true meaning for ritual
actions. The task is what the fathers of the church
perceived it to be—the cultivation of the imagination
and memory of the neophytes. — Mary Collins[1]

This quotation might appear, on the surface, to have a
limited application. Most of us have a rather strict interpretation of the word "neophyte." It is a challenge for all of us
and an appeal to our humility to begin to consider everyone
a neophyte to some degree, precisely because we are in a
continual process of being made new in Christ. We awake
each day with the gift of a fresh set of eyes with which to
gaze upon our world and the people in it. God never ceases
to work in our lives. We are continuously presented with
the possibility of things made new. We will always be
neophytes in some sense of the word in that there will
always be something to learn, some way to grow, some way

---

[1] Collins, *Worship: Renewal to Practice*, 273-4.

to be formed and transformed in Christ. When we lose our sense of being made new, when we cease to identify with being a neophyte, we have lost the passion and vigor that are so vital for Christian life. Let me begin with a story, which may perhaps say all that needs to be said about the direction we should take.

Following a stimulating discussion about where our renewal efforts were headed, one of the participants in the discussion had one of those "Aha!" moments. He said that he was beginning to realize that buying a two-thousand-dollar altar was not the solution. It was dawning on him that what was needed was honest attention to the people who come to worship every week, honest attention to the liturgical ministers who serve faithfully. He said that it is so much easier to go out and buy something than to begin the slow process of really working with people. No gimmicks, no instant solutions, no magic tricks to bring us into a deeper life in Christ that our liturgies promise us.

We who are working in renewal must become midwives, assisting in the often slow, ongoing process of the birthing of ourselves in Christ anew each time we gather to celebrate liturgy. Again, there is paradox here because, even though it can be slow and painful, we must cherish the utter joy at each sign of new life, each stirring, each step of the process. We must learn to notice the delicate nuances of the Spirit's gentle guidance, to support, encourage and give thanks for these movements. We must hold hands firmly when we move through the transitions of our birth. We must learn to breathe into the holy rhythm of God's continuing revelation. We must be patient during the times when our labor seems to be at an utter standstill or worse, when we seem to be moving backward.

Recovering Basic Elements

Several elements basic to worship must be recovered and encouraged if renewal is to be the rekindling of passion—passion for our faith, passion for our journeys, passion for the God who so loves us.

Silence

We need to have a basic comfort level with silence—remember God's exhortation to "be still and know that I am God" (Ps 46:11). The General Instruction is so specific about silence during liturgy that we would be remiss if we did not attend to it. The function of silence...

> depends on the time it occurs in each part of the celebration. Thus at the Penitential Rite and again after the invitation to prayer, all recollect themselves; at the conclusion of a reading or the homily, all meditate briefly on what has been heard; after Communion, all praise God in silent prayer (GI, n. 23).

Silence cannot be taught, but it is possible to model it and invite the community into it.

Reverence

We need to recover reverence. "Reverence" comes directly from the Latin word *reverentia*. Reverence is a feeling or attitude of deep respect, love, awe and esteem. We express reverence in many ways, especially through our body language: bows, curtsies, genuflection. Being reverent toward someone can be as simple as a nod of the head, an acknowledgment of their presence. Hospitality ministers have the opportunity to model reverence as they greet people upon their arrival in the church vestibule.

Watch people as they enter a church—there is a definite lack of reverence among many. I think reverence is absent because we've not modeled it well in the last two decades and because our culture does not place a high value on it. I am not advocating stiff-necked, formal comportment—reverence has an elegance about it that is beautiful to behold.

> How lovely is your dwelling place, O LORD of hosts!
> My soul yearns and pines for the courts of the LORD
> (Ps 84:2-3).

Part of the beauty we find in our churches—in the assembly, in the environment, in the liturgical celebration—comes from the reverence expressed in them. Something was lost when English was found. A certain casualness has arisen that is detrimental to our expressions of reverence. We would *never* presume or expect anyone to learn verbal expressions on their own. Why should expressions of reverence be any different?

Senses

We need to involve all our senses in whatever we do. For most of us, a forty-five-minute presentation, even one that is extraordinary, drifts into the obscure recesses of the brain all too quickly. At best, we will remember a stray phrase or thought. What will remain, however, is the sight of a simple wooden cross, the smell of incense, the feel of water sprinkled upon your face, the taste of the wine, the sound of a lone bell. For some reason, we recall these tangible experiences far more easily, and they have a greater potential for jarring our memories and drawing us into their mystery.

Imagination

We need to rouse our imaginations. We are a culture on automatic pilot. How often do we let our imaginations roam, interact with a symbol and tease our memories into life? How often do we just spend a few moments telling stories to our friends and our children? One of the fruits born from the use of our imagination is the creation of much-needed language that more accurately describes our life experiences in the twentieth century. We see some changes beginning to occur in the emergence of new images: web, net, story, weaving, circle, process, journey, stewardship. In service of our worship, "imagination serves to transform human behavior and thus serves the process of human conversion."[2]

Developing Basic Actions

Several things we do during liturgy enhance our public worship. They are basic, yet many people are unfamiliar with them or have overlooked their contribution to meaningful worship.

Communal Prayer

We have stated that liturgy is prayer. As basic as prayer might appear to be, it is a relationship between God and the people of God that requires a certain amount of discipline and attentiveness. When we pray aloud together, we must begin to notice how it is different from other oral exercises. When we pray silently together, we must begin to notice how it is different from praying silently by our-

---

[2] Fink, "Imagination and Worship," *New Dictionary of Sacramental Worship*, 593.

selves. And, although Jesus was speaking primarily of personal prayer in the Sermon on the Mount, it is wise to take to heart his plea: "Do not behave like hypocrites...do not rattle on like pagans" (Mt 5:5, 7). Jesus' disciples were wise enough to ask Jesus how to pray (Lk 11:1); it would be wise for us to ask as well.

Reflection

Reflection is simply letting our experiences tell us their story. We need to resist the temptation to "acquire" experiences like trophies, which is the cultural norm. Reflection is taking the time to be with our experiences, in all their many nuances, in their delicate layers of meaning, in subtleties that are initially hidden. Reflection is about noticing what is happening. In our noticing we discover the God that has always been there, the God who has never left our side.

A simple process might help you begin to be comfortable with reflection:

◊ Begin by asking yourself what part of the
   liturgy grabbed your attention on a particular
   day; it could be an object, action, word or a
   simple moment.

◊ Continue by noticing all that you can about
   that part.

◊ Ask yourself how it touched you and why.

◊ Notice your response to that part.

◊ What story did it tell you and how did you
   feel about it?

Again, this noticing must be done gently and with an understanding that part of your experience will always remain mystery *by its very nature.* This is not dissection;

it is cooperation. We must follow the lead of the Spirit in our reflections. To invite reflection is to make full, conscious and active participation possible.

Willingness to Share

Once we have reflected on a certain part of the liturgy, the next step is to share with others. The fruit of our experience is always meant to be shared in some way at some time. The sharing of our reflections deepens them and makes them more real to us. Sharing can be done one-on-one or it can be done in a group. When done in a group in a sensitive manner, the members will realize many benefits. Upon hearing reflections that are similar to our own, we feel comforted and affirmed; so often we feel unsure of our own experiences. Upon hearing reflections that are different from our own, our eyes are opened to the many colors that are present in the same prism.

As we share, our awe and appreciation of liturgy grows and deepens. Again, as with anything else, this sharing reveals a negative side when comparison and judgment become part of the process. Thus, sharing, especially in a group, must be done in such a way as to discourage comparison and judgments, to the extent that this is possible.

Organizing Programs and Projects

Beyond the basic elements and actions, here are some specific projects and programs that would complement and further liturgical renewal in a community setting. These programs could be organized as a joint effort between liturgy and education committees or liturgy and spiritual life committees. The projects could be organized in such a way that they are an ongoing part of the community for an extended period of time. Again, as was stated at the outset, each community has its own needs, resources and limitations that cannot be specifically addressed or considered on a scale such as this.

Discovering Personal Symbols

Following the invitation that was made in Chapter 5 to search out personal symbols, an evening devoted to symbols might be beneficial. It is a starting point for recovering the energy and story in each of our liturgical symbols. You might utilize the following suggestions:

◊ Begin with a short explanation about what symbols are.

◊ Presenters could share several of their own personal symbols so that those who are participating have a sense of what they are looking for in their own lives.

◊ Provide quiet time so that the participants have an opportunity to identify and reflect on one of their own personal symbols.

◊ Follow with small group process so that personal symbols can be shared.

◊ Close by linking the energy and process of personal symbol to the energy and story of liturgical symbols. While the surface content differs, the process and the end point—the face of profound and utter mystery—are the same.

Working with Liturgical Symbols

We saw an example of praying with liturgical symbols in Chapter 5. The elements of silence, reverence, senses and

imagination need to be present in an evening of prayer such
as this. Modeling prayer, encouraging reflection and developing a willingness to share must be incorporated as well.
While this may sound somewhat intimidating, do not underestimate the effectiveness of good modeling. Much can
be communicated if the presenters for the evening model
well—if, instead of talking about praying, they do it. If,
instead of talking about reflection, they do it. Again, there
needs to be a balance—some teaching, some modeling.

Praying with liturgical symbols could take any or all of
the methods used in Chapter 5:

◊ providing Scripture passages that refer to a
   particular symbol

◊ praying quietly with the Scripture

◊ sharing reflections

◊ involving the senses in some kind of action
   around the symbol

This method engages our imaginations; it also involves a
willingness to work with the symbol and follow its lead.

Telling Your Own Stories

The threads we weave in liturgy are identified in Chapter
2: prayer, sacrament, meal, celebration, story, liberation.
Liturgy and life are in a constant process of intersection.
We have looked in detail at these threads as they are
experienced in the liturgical setting. It would be helpful to
look at these same threads as they run through our daily
lives in the personal setting.

Spending an evening working with the following questions will help you to connect your own stories to the
process of liturgy.

◊ When has an experience in the daily comings and goings of your life become prayer (as distinguished from saying prayers)? Become an intimate relationship with the divine?

◊ When has an experience in your life become sacrament, become an intimate revelation of the divine?

◊ When has a meal assumed a quality of mystery, a quality of "more than?"

◊ When, during the course of an ordinary evening dinner, have you come to recognize Jesus in the breaking of the bread at the table in your own dining room?

◊ When have you come to experience liberation in a simple exercise, in a project at your workplace, in a favor for a friend?

Jesus' saving act is woven into the fabric of our lives and our liturgies. We need to share our stories with each other. They come *alive* in the sharing. Connections that seemed vague become much more concrete. Liturgy is an intimate expression of all that we experience in our own lives, and our lives are an intimate expression of all that we celebrate in liturgy. No longer will our public worship be something "out there" with little or no meaning to the rest of our lives. The more we see these connections, the more we will be able to weave the threads of liturgy and the threads of our own lives together—the myriad experiences of both will come to be woven into one seamless piece of fabric that is nothing less than the divine revelation and grace of God in our lives.

Praying with Scripture

Listening to Scripture is far more than simply hearing words read out loud in the same way that proclaiming Scripture is far more than simply reading aloud. To assume that we know how to do either would be foolish. As listeners, we need to be invited to enter into the Scripture passage being read aloud, to actually identify with a character or action. The paralytic on the mat (Mk 2:1-12) has many characters and a great deal of action. It is an ideal Scripture with which to begin.

It is helpful to place the people in the scene by appealing to all their senses: suggest that they feel the heat of the day, the crush of the crowd; hear the noise of all the people; picture the home in their mind; see the four carrying the mat. Once the people are inside the Scripture setting, a clear proclamation of the Word is all that is needed. When people become familiar with this type of listening, Scripture becomes alive in a way that amazes most.

We can be taught how to listen for a word, image or series of words that seem to have more energy than the rest, that seem to leap out and grab us. This is a little different from entering a piece of action-packed Scripture. Isaiah 55 has many images that might leap out—come to the water, seek the Lord, scoundrels forsake their way, rain and snow come down and water the earth, my word goes forth from my mouth, mountains and hills shall break out in song. We need to be encouraged to go back to those words over the course of the day or week, to allow them to soak into our hearts as rain soaks into dry ground. If there is an energy or pull around them, they have a message to tell us. During every liturgy, we must honor the Scripture proclaimed through attentive listening with an open heart. To do so is to honor Christ himself, who

"is the center and fullness of all Scripture, as he is of the entire liturgy. Thus the Scriptures are the living

waters from which all who seek life and salvation
must drink" (LI, n. 5).

Weaving

If you resonate with the metaphor of liturgy as a weaving
process (see Chapter 2), you might consider involving your
community in a weaving project. On your loom you will
weave together the people in your community, your community's experiences of liturgy, and each member's experiences in daily life.

Choose either a small hand-held loom that can be passed
from person to person over the course of a single evening,
or use a larger loom for a weaving project that is part of an
extended program of liturgical renewal in your community.

For those unfamiliar with weaving, the first threads
placed on the loom are the long, vertical threads or *warp*
threads. They will represent the people in your community—the people God so loves. Then you will begin to
weave the *woof* or *weft* threads, and you will see God's
presence among and within you as it is revealed in liturgy
and in life.

Silently weave the threads of liturgy and life in and out,
passing the shuttle noiselessly among all the threads that
represent the people in your community. It will be a holy
process.

You may want to use colors of thread that you feel best
represent these elements of liturgy (discussed in detail in
Chapter 2):

◊ Prayer threads — the holy relationship of God
  and God's people—weaving in and out.
  There is a gentleness to the process.

◊ Sacramental threads — God's presence
  revealed in worship—weaving in and out.
  There is a rhythm to the motion.

◊ Meal threads — Jesus' body and blood broken and poured out to save us—weaving in and out. There is a beauty in watching many hands move tirelessly.

◊ Celebration threads — how much you have to be thankful for; God is so good—weaving in and out. There is a gracefulness to the pattern beginning to emerge.

◊ Story threads — the story of your formation and transformation as a covenant community—weaving in and out. There is a peace in seeing the threads of community and the threads of liturgy become one whole.

◊ Liberation threads — Jesus has come to set the captives free—weaving in and out. There is a joy in seeing this project come to fruition.

Then begin to weave the threads of each member's life experience onto the loom. Your personal experiences are shared, held and woven together in such a way that you see how intimately connected all experience is. Following are some examples.

◊ Walking in the forest — relationship with God intimately alive. Weaving in and out, prayer threads complement your communal prayer.

◊ Weeping with a friend — God's presence revealed in a tender moment. Weaving in and out, sacramental threads are found in an unexpected place.

◊ An ordinary meal with your family — Jesus is at table with you. Weaving in and out, meal threads mirror those found in liturgy.

◊ A high school graduation — you have so
   much to be thankful for. Weaving in and out,
   celebration threads blend into your liturgical
   celebrations.

◊ Sharing stories over tea — you come to know
   yourselves in the process. Weaving in and
   out, story threads help you discover God's
   ways in your lives.

◊ Working in a soup kitchen — you come to
   see Jesus in the homeless people whom you
   serve. Weaving in and out, liberation threads
   are brought out into the world.

When all is said and done, you will have woven liturgy
and life together. The process is a holy process; the fabric
is the fabric of God's steadfast presence in all that you do
and all that you are. And, as you stand back to gaze upon
your handiwork, you begin to see how it is, in the words
of Meister Eckhart, that you "are to be changed into God
and sometime made One with [God]." Your weaving has
become that reality, an already but not yet that will always
be in process.

Cross-Cultural Dialogue

It would prove interesting (and perhaps a little dangerous) to gather people from different ethnic backgrounds
and economic classes to discuss their responses to both the
passage in Acts 2 about the ideals of the early Christian
community and the passage from the parable quoted in
Chapter 7.

Liturgy is conversion. As such, it extends far beyond the
confines of the walls of the church building; it is a conversion that moves far beyond the individual realm.

> Personal conversion does demand the
> transformation of social structures. But the

transformation of social structures is also required
for personal conversion. The Gospel calls us to
work for both simultaneously.[3]

We must pay attention to our social structures, to our
culture. Opening up dialogue between different groups of
people is an excellent way to start.

◊ How does each interpret and react to these
two passages?

◊ How do we begin to adopt this ideal
first-century Christian life to the twentieth
century? Can it be done?

◊ What does this ideal look like in our current
era?

Liturgy calls us to greater loving service, to more equita-
ble social systems, to greater justice, to the living of a life
firmly rooted in the *sacrifice* of Jesus. To the extent that
we ignore this call, our participation in liturgy will be
incomplete, if not completely lacking.

We cannot engage fully if we do not want to hear the
underlying message of every liturgical celebration—"feed
my lambs...tend my sheep...feed my sheep...follow me" (Jn
21:15-19). This is a command with no qualifications. It calls
for our response, even unto death, be it literal or figurative.
When we cannot hear this, we become like children with
eyes screwed tightly shut, hands clapped firmly over ears,
crying, "We can't hear you." We become unlikely candi-
dates for mature Christian participation in liturgy.

Cross-cultural dialogue and twinning of parishes help us
to touch the inequalities and understand the injustices of
existing social, economic, political, and religious systems.
Commitment to correcting these inequalities and injustices
will come alive in our hearts. Participation in liturgy will

---

3 Walter Conn, *Christian Conversion*, 204.

deepen our commitment to these efforts. It is a process that comes full circle over and over again: liturgy–commitment–dialogue–commitment–liturgy. When we can begin to formulate a realistic sense of the ideal Christian life in today's language, we can begin to work concretely toward that ideal. This is done most effectively when we are in touch with many different cultures and economic classes.

Working with the Elements of Worship

I have purposely tried to present recommendations and ideas that focus on working with the people and their God at prayer together. All the bells and whistles, all the adaptations to the ritual, all the liturgical team preparations (if you are fortunate enough to have such cooperative efforts in your community) will not help if the people are not there or they are asleep. They need to be awake, they need to recognize their hunger, they need to touch their innermost desire to become all that God intends them to be—beings delightfully loved by and in love with God.

At the same time, it is important to continue to work with the elements of worship. There are a number of ways we can do this:

Liturgical Practice

We need to continue assessing our liturgical practices in light of the vision of Vatican II. A careful, thoughtful reading and understanding of the documents is critical, at the very least the CSL (1963) and the GI (1969). If issues such as those mentioned in Chapter 2 still exist in your parishes, what can be done to correct them? Some questions that your community might ask itself include:

◊ If bread alone is offered at Communion,
   what can be done to make both species

available? If bread is not broken, how can
you begin to organize an effort to make it
happen?

◊ When are announcements made? If they are
made before Mass, after the homily, before
Communion (or, in a creative vein, played
subliminally through the sound system
during the entire celebration—who knows
what's next?), it is important to know that
the proper time is after Communion (GI 123).

◊ If homilies are not preached to the readings,
why not? When the readings are not opened
up by the homily, the critical bridge
between Liturgy of the Word and Liturgy of
the Eucharist is absent.

Liturgy done sloppily, without care, incorrectly, without
prior thought and planning dishonors God and creates
unnecessary distractions to our prayer.

Liturgical Gesture

A bow should look like a bow. It should be reverent,
intentional, graceful, generous and unhurried. This goes for
all liturgical gestures; there is no harm in demonstrating and
practicing. We are often uncomfortable with gesture not
only because we are uncomfortable with our bodies, but
also because we just do not know how to do it well. A little
practice goes a long way toward easing feelings of awk-
wardness and self-consciousness.

Liturgical Symbols

Bread should look like bread. If we are going to do a Rite
of Blessing, all the people should be able to feel water on

their faces or heads. Much was said and done about this aspect of symbol during the early period of renewal, but we seem to have become stingy again with our symbols' representation and execution. This is a basic principle and one that is not difficult to implement for the most part. However, it is one that is too often overlooked. Keep in mind that EACW (n. 15) states that,

> renewal requires the opening up of our symbols, especially the fundamental ones of bread and wine, water, oil, the laying on of hands, until we can experience all of them as authentic and appreciate their symbolic value.

Music and Environment

We must attend to the environment and to music. If they are ignored or overdone, they will be distractions to prayer. Care must be taken that both complement the season of the year and the readings of the day. It is extremely important to read the documents that pertain to these areas, most notably Environment and Art in Catholic Worship (1978), Music in Catholic Worship (1972), and Liturgical Music Today (1982).

Catechesis for Worship

We must continue to seek out quality education for both the ordained and the non-ordained. The call for this in the documents is clear. John Baldovin points this out simply and succinctly, "We tend to forget that, like speaking a language, liturgy is something we learn."[4] It isn't automatic and it isn't once for all of time. "Catechesis" has become an important word in the last twenty years; the learning must be more than the basic teaching of doctrine. Instead of

---

[4] Baldovin, *Worship: Church and Renewal*, 194.

going into a long, detailed explanation of what is involved in catechesis,[5] a small story will provide an illustration of the process.

In discussing what is essential for the formation of presiders, one priest observed that they first have to be taught how to pick up the chalice, how far off the altar they should lift it, how long to hold it, and when it should be put down. Then, they need to pray through every one of those motions until the prayer is *in their blood, in every part of them*. The final step is to go back through the process once again. The presider is formed and transformed; in this simple action of elevating the cup, subject and object become part of a greater whole, a process that cannot help but resonate throughout the entire praying community. This is a catechesis for all—assembly, liturgical ministers, presiders.

These basic ideas have been around for a long time. For some reason, we have stubbornly overlooked many of them, or only attended to them when the mood was right. We need to assent to their ideals and commit to an implementation that is consistent and ongoing. We must approach renewal in a balanced fashion, working with both how the community prays and reflects and how the ritual itself is celebrated and "taught": its objects, actions and words, its environment and music. When we are able to attend to both the community and the ritual, our renewal will be a rekindling of passion.

---

5 Gilbert Ostdiek explains catechesis clearly in his article, "Catechesis, Liturgical," *New Dictionary of Sacramental Worship*, 163-172.

CHAPTER 9

How Do We Get There?

Christians are to care for one another as well as for
other sister and brother humans;
and this care is a key manifestation, or sacrament,
of the divine care. — Bernard Cooke[1]

We must begin to identify the liturgical work that we do
with the work of pastoral care, whether we find ourselves
leaders of renewal efforts in our community, members of
the assembly or servants of it—presiders, music ministers,
eucharistic ministers, cantors, hospitality ministers, altar
servers, environmental ministers, lectors, cross bearers.
We can be about nothing if we are not first and always
centered in God. A look at pastoral care will provide us with
the framework to do just that.

In whatever we do for and with each other, there is a
specific, underlying essence that is shared by all—this is the
heart of pastoral care. St. Paul names this essence clearly:

"There are different gifts but the same Spirit; there
are different ministries but the same Lord; there are

---

[1] Cooke, "Sacraments," *New Dictionary of Sacramental Worship,*
1122.

different works but the same God who
accomplishes all of them in everyone" (1 Cor
12:4-6).

This essence permeates all ministry work, including pastoral and liturgical ministry, spiritual direction and pastoral
counseling. All ministry has this underlying essence, and it
has a unifying goal as well: "increasing human wholeness
centered in the Spirit. Each function [ministry] can be an
instrument of growth and healing, a channel of pastoral
caring."[2]

Pastoral Care Giving in Our Ministries

In reviewing definitions of pastoral care, many authors
seem to classify it as a separate area of ministry, on a
horizontal plane that includes spiritual direction and pastoral counseling, liturgical and pastoral ministry.[3] I would
contend, however, that pastoral care is not something
separate, above, or side by side the other ministries. It is
not another type of ministry. *Pastoral care is the awareness and expression of the essence of God that permeates
and informs all areas of ministry.* This awareness of God
distinguishes Christian ministry from whatever secular
counterparts might exist (the existence of secular counterparts is particularly obvious within the areas of pastoral
counseling and pastoral ministry).

Each of us might ask ourselves: Where and how is God
revealed in my particular ministry? God is revealed in our
midst...

◊ ...when we form community.

---

[2] Clinebell, *Basic Types of Pastoral Care and Counseling,* 38.

[3] Charles Topper, "Definitions of Pastoral Care," unpublished paper, 1.

◊ ...when we see mutuality in our service.

◊ ...when we work toward inclusiveness.

◊ ...when we are guided by the vision of Christ.

◊ ...when we act from a place that is oriented
toward growth.

◊ ...when we are able to support and challenge
in love.

◊ ...when we are able to reflect with faith on
our personal experiences.

When we see ourselves as pastoral care givers in whatever we do, we are able to name and also be guided by this
essence, this presence of God. Seeing this, we also recognize the initiating action of God. When this presence and
action is both tacitly and overtly expressed in and through
community, mutuality, inclusiveness, vision, orientation
toward growth, support/challenge, and reflection, Christian qualities and virtues will become an increasingly visible
part of our ministry. The Pauline writer sees these qualities
and virtues clearly:

> Because you are God's chosen ones, holy and
> beloved, clothe yourselves with heartfelt mercy,
> with kindness, humility, meekness, and patience.
> Bear with one another; forgive whatever grievances
> you have against one another. Forgive as the Lord
> has forgiven you. Over all these virtues put on love,
> which binds the rest together and makes them
> perfect. Christ's peace must reign in your hearts,
> since as members of the one body you have been
> called to that peace. Dedicate yourselves to
> thankfulness. Let the word of Christ, rich as it is,
> dwell in you. In wisdom made perfect, instruct and
> admonish one another...Whatever you do...do it in
> the name of the Lord Jesus. Give thanks to God the
> Father through him (Col 3:12-17).

Components of Pastoral Care

The foregoing passage from Colossians sums up some of the most important components of pastoral care. We must bring an understanding of these components and their corresponding Christian virtues/fruits into all of our efforts of liturgical renewal. We also need to find a willingness to bring them into our own lives. When we clothe ourselves with the mind of Christ, which is what the Pauline writer is describing in this passage, we become more effective ministers, be it in one-on-one relationships or in working with the community.

Community and Covenantal Promise

This component is perhaps the most important one. We examined it in great detail in Chapter 3. When we gather, we form not just a community, but a community in covenant with God. This community can be as large as a five-hundred-member assembly who has come together to worship or as small as two people who meet for spiritual direction or counseling. A deeply rooted sense of covenant brings a rich dimension to community, whether large or small. God's promise and invitation to us to be covenant community is revealed in the First Testament: "I will sprinkle clean water upon you...I will give you a new heart...I will put my spirit within you...you shall be my people and I will be your God" (Ez 36:25-28).

The Christian Scriptures broaden the vision of this community: "Where two or three are gathered in my name, there am I in their midst" (Mt 18:20). Within community is the promise of renewal in the real presence of Jesus. "Ministers serve the community...by cultivating a keen sensitivity to God's continuing action in others' lives."[4]

---

[4] Duffy, *Real Presence*, 193.

God's desire forms this community; Christ's presence transforms it; the Spirit's gifts empower it. "It exists for partner-
ship in God's creative work, God's work of judgment and
governance, and God's work of redemption and liberation."[5] We are bound together in love as Body of Christ.
This is our community; this is the covenantal promise and
gift God has made to God's people.

Reflecting on the following questions may help you evaluate your community as a covenantal community.

◊ What does God's promise to make us God's
  people mean to you? What does it mean to
  be in a covenant with God? How do you feel
  about this promise and covenant?

◊ How does Christian community differ from
  other groups to which you belong?

◊ What words, images, and/or pictures come
  to mind when you sit with the words "Body
  of Christ"?

◊ How does a firm, clear sense of being the
  Body of Christ enhance your worship
  personally? Communally? How does your
  worship enhance your sense of being Body
  of Christ?

◊ What obstacles exist in your community that
  might prevent you from forming a true
  covenantal community—a connected, living
  breathing Body of Christ? How might you go
  about removing the obstacles?

---

[5] Fowler, *Faith Development and Pastoral Care*, 35.

Mutuality and Humility

A well-developed sense of mutuality is important in ministry where burn-out and frustration are frequently experienced on many different levels.

> The church teaches and shares its corporate
> wisdom through many different ministries. But the
> church is also taught by the child, the adult, the
> neophyte...mutuality is a characteristic of every
> ministry.[6]

No ministry is one-directional. In virtually every situation, at some level and in some way, everyone is ministered to. "In the measure you give you shall receive, and more besides" (Mk 4:24). Caregivers bring to their ministry their need to be of help and service. Their need is met by those who need them. Beyond the basic need level is an entire level of exchange: those who teach are taught; those who listen, learn; those who give are given. We need each other! This sense of mutuality gives birth to the humility Paul asks of us. It also gives birth to a healthy respect and appreciation of the other that often gets lost when we are feeling overwhelmed by the demands of our ministry, whatever form it takes.

Reflecting on the following questions may help you evaluate your experience of mutuality and humility:

◊ What words, pictures, and/or images come
  to mind when you sit with the word
  "mutuality"? With "humility"?

◊ If mutuality and humility are difficult or
  uncomfortable words for you, what might be
  causing the discomfort? What might help
  you to become more comfortable with them?

---

[6] Hovda, *There Are Different Ministries*, 8.

◊ As a member of the worshipping
    community, which of your needs are met
    when you come to worship together? How
    do the others in the assembly serve you and
    how do you serve them?

◊ If you are in a liturgical ministry, which of
    your needs are met when you minister to
    others? How do you feel about your ministry?

◊ How does a firm, clear sense of mutuality
    and humility enhance your worship
    personally? Communally? How does your
    worship enhance your sense of mutuality
    and humility?

Inclusiveness and Reconciliation

Our scriptural tradition clearly articulates the sense of
inclusiveness that we should carry into all of our ministry
work.

> There is but one body and one Spirit, just as there is
> but one hope given all of you by your call. There is
> one Lord, one faith, one baptism; one God and
> Father of all, who is over all, and works through all,
> and is in all (Eph 4:4-6).

There is no mention of exclusion for any reason here, no
mention of complex hierarchy, no mention of a system
which judges some as less worthy of invitation.

Our ability to openly include and accept is possible only
when there has been reconciliation, only when we have
been able "to bear with one another and forgive whatever
grievances we might have." As we receive this forgiveness
and reconciliation, we learn to be more forgiving and
reconciling. Barriers and impediments to relationship fall

away. We are moved to accept and then to include.[7] Jesus' own example of inviting the most lowly to share at table with him can serve as our own example: "If Jesus ate with sinners as a witness to God's offer of reconciliation, how can his Church do any less?...[we must] reach out creatively to the 'unacceptable' and the 'undesirable'..."[8] as part of our call to serve.

Reflecting on the following questions may help you evaluate your community's experience of inclusiveness and reconciliation:

◊ What words, pictures, and/or images come to mind when you sit with the word "inclusiveness"? With "reconciliation"?

◊ What types of people do you find yourself judging in any way? When you make a judgment (negative or positive) about a person or persons, what happens in your relationship with that individual or group?

◊ Are there certain types of people your community does not include or includes in a limited way? Why does this happen?

◊ When someone or some group makes you feel included, how does that make you feel?

◊ How does a firm, clear sense of inclusiveness and reconciliation enhance your worship personally? Communally? How does your

---

[7] I propose an interesting parallel here between this statement and one made by Sebastian Moore in his book, *Let This Mind Be In You*. He states on p. xi that "we only desire [include/reconcile] out of a sense of being desirable [included/reconciled]. We only feel desirable [included/reconciled] absolutely because we are absolutely desired [included/reconciled]."

[8] Duffy, *Real Presence*, 151.

worship enhance your sense of inclusiveness and reconciliation?

Vision and Prophecy

Forming a faith-inspired vision of those people for whom we care is critical to our work. The vision is neither complicated nor sophisticated; its very simplicity baffles most. The vision involves two dimensions—that of the individual and that of the community. Our vision of individuals is well put by St. Paul: "the life I live now is not my own; Christ is living in me. I still live my human life, but it is a life of faith in the Son of God, who loved me and gave himself for me" (Gal 2:20). We must embrace this vision of Christ living in each of us; it must become the vision that we have of each other. How different we would feel, how different would our actions be if we allowed this vision to inform all that we do.

Our vision of community, as we saw in Chapter 3, is one of the Body of Christ: "all the members may be concerned for one another. If one member suffers, all the members suffer with it; if one member is honored, all the members share its joy. You then, are the body of Christ" (1 Cor 12:25-27).

As pastoral care givers within liturgical ministry and leadership, we have a responsibility to treat each individual we meet according to that vision. When we greet each person, it is Christ whom we greet as well. "God is not to be found in isolated individualism then, but in others."[9]

As we treat each other as Christ-like, we become more Christ-like. When we view the community as the Body of Christ, our reverence and respect will grow for a people who have come together in Jesus' name. As we act in light of this vision—a vision that we can translate into a sense that

---

[9]   Walter Conn, *Christian Conversion*, 237.

"all of life is or can be theophany"[10]—the vision becomes a self-fulfilling prophecy. In one hand we hold the prophetic call that we are to become Christ and Body of Christ *in the future.* In the other hand, we hold the vision that we, as individuals, are Christ and that we, as community, are Body of Christ *in the present moment.* When we act in light of the vision, the prophecy becomes a deeper reality for an ever-increasing number of people.

Reflecting on the following questions may help you evaluate your experience of vision and prophecy:

◊ What words, pictures, and/or images come to mind when you sit with the word "vision"? With "prophecy"?

◊ Recall a time when you thought you couldn't do something and someone thought you could and was certain you would. Was that helpful? If so, how?

◊ Think of a time when you had a clear sense of what you were doing or where you were going. How did that help you move forward?

◊ When have you experienced another person being Christ-like to you? How did that affect your attitude and behavior toward him/her?

◊ How do a firm, clear sense of vision and prophecy enhance your worship personally? Communally? How does your worship enhance your sense of vision and prophecy?

---

[10] Carroll and Dyckman, *Inviting the Mystic, Supporting the Prophet,* 20.

Orientation toward Growth and Transcendence

This orientation enables us to view the people with whom we work as people in search of a different way of being. Through this orientation, we see the human being as a creature in search of the transcendent[11]; in our Judaeo-Christian tradition, we name the transcendent "God."

> What we are looking for is a way of experiencing the world that will open to us the transcendent that informs it, and at the same time forms ourselves within it. That is what people want. That is what the soul asks for.[12]

In our work in liturgical renewal, we must begin to look at all the various needs, tasks and issues that occupy us as openings into growth, not as demands to be met and pathologies to be corrected. It is generally believed by most developmental theorists that the movement from place to place is often precipitated by crisis, which is translated by the Chinese as "opportunity." Liturgy brings us into the heart of this opportunity over and over again by challenging us to greater honesty, by challenging us to see who and where we are now and who and where God is calling us to be. Resolution of the crisis brought about by these challenges is about conversion; resolution often moves us to a place in our journeys that is more transcendent than the previous one, to a place where we live in greater awareness of and harmony with God.

As pastoral care givers, the view of crisis resolution as a potential for growth, as movement into greater self-aware-

---

[11] Walter Conn's *Christian Conversion* is devoted to the theme that human beings are naturally transcendent beings. His assessment of all developmental theories is that they move the person toward greater ability to realize self-transcendency, which he calls "a norm of maturity" (page 69).

[12] Campbell, *Power of Myth*, 53.

ness, autonomy, and transcendence can positively effect
our view of the work that we do and the people we serve.
Perception (negative and positive) tends to be contagious
and self-fulfilling. A secure, clear, informed orientation
toward growth is invaluable for any pastoral care giver.

Reflecting on the following questions may help you evaluate your experience of growth and transcendence:

◊ What words, pictures, and/or images come
to mind when you sit with the word
"problem"? With "crisis"?

◊ What words, pictures, and/or images come
to mind when you sit with the word
"opportunity"? With "growth"?

◊ Name a time in your own life when a crisis
brought you to a better place.

◊ When do liturgical celebrations precipitate
crisis?

◊ How has liturgy helped your community
move to a better place, to a place that is
more inclusive, more mutual, more just, in
terms of being with other people and in
other situations?

Support/Challenge and Liberation

Our ability to both support and challenge is one of the
many paradoxes that are part of living a life based on
Christian faith. As ministers, we support those whom we
serve, but at the same time we also need to promote an
environment in which the people we serve are free to
challenge themselves as well as accept challenge from
others when their feelings and behavior appear to be incon-
sistent with the gospel message. "An honest listener also

knows when to confront. Active, compassionate listening helps to unmask illusions [and] indicate inconsistencies."[13]

As ministers who serve the community as a whole, we need to present the gospel message in a way that moves people to action, not complacency. "Praise of God that is not coupled with service is an abomination...the Church must spell out, in positive terms...what that commitment concretely means..."[14]

This component of pastoral care involves supporting people as they struggle to understand and then answer God's call to them as individuals and as community; it also involves challenging them when they grow complacent and satisfied with ritual alone. In Jesus, we have the perfect example of this component. He supports through his healing and his love; he challenges through his many exhortations to the people to take up their cross (Mk 8:34), sell their possessions and give to the poor (Mt 19:21) and to serve (Lk 22:27).

When we respond to caring support and honest challenge, we move beyond our concern with material possessions and self-absorption into loving service of others. What we experience is liberation from past wounds and current values that are false and misleading. Healed from our wounds and obsessions, we may hear the gospel message more clearly and experience its transforming power more deeply.

Reflecting on the following questions may help you evaluate your experience of support/challenge and liberation:

◊ What words, pictures, and/or images come
to mind when you sit with the word
"support"? With "challenge"?

---

[13] Carroll and Dyckman, *Inviting the Mystic, Supporting the Prophet*, 24.

[14] Duffy, *Real Presence*, 194.

◊ When have you welcomed and been helped by another's support? When have you been helped by another's challenge?

◊ How does liturgy both support and challenge you personally? Communally?

◊ What would help you be more open to receiving both support and challenge from others in your community? What would help your community be more open to receiving support and challenge from other communities?

Reflection and Wisdom

Reflection upon our life experience is like fertilizer in the soil—it will bring the experience into its greatest life and purpose; it allows the experience to bear its fruit, the wisdom hidden within it. This is as true about our liturgical experience as it is about other experiences. Through *reflected experience*, which constitutes our meaning-seeking, our faith is deepened and strengthened. Personal reflection by any minister, regardless of his/her situation, is a necessary component for effective ministry. "A calm review of experience as it relates to the sources of faith, the people who are being cared for, and one's day-to-day relationship with God is essential."[15]

Reflection has been a large part of my training and practice as a spiritual director. The closest definition that Webster has for "reflection" (which I would define as a form of art) is "a thought, idea or opinion formed or a remark made as a result of meditation." Used in the context of pastoral care, reflection is more than thinking about something. Thinking about something means, "I am here, and what I

---

[15] Stone, *Word of God and Pastoral Care*, 36.

am thinking about is out there." There is a sense of subject
(I) and object (what I am thinking about), with separation
and distance between the two. "Thinking" is standing at
the edge of a lake, thinking about swimming. "Reflection"
is suddenly finding yourself in the water swimming. There
is a world of difference.

I recently heard the word "savor" and was struck by the
relationship between reflecting and savoring. Reflecting on
an experience will show that there is something to savor
in everything that happens. Even in painful experiences,
there is something to savor, to delight in if we allow
ourselves the chance to reflect deeply. If we remain open
to the process of reflection, if we allow ourselves simply
"to be" with the experience, we will discover the funda-
mental truth and wisdom about all that happens: God truly
is with us in all manner of things. Not only is God with us
but, in the words of Julian of Norwich,

> ...you will see for yourself, that all things will be
> well...it is God's will that we should know in
> general that all will be well...[16]

We must begin to reflect on what has happened to us
before we can work with and for others. Reflection allows
us to savor our experience. Our faith is formed, transformed and enlivened; in the process our passion is rekin-
dled and reclaimed. We can learn various facts about
Christian tradition and ritual, but these, in and of themselves, will not constitute faith. When we reflect on and
savor our experience in the light of Scripture and tradition,
we will come to deeper faith and wisdom.[17] Wisdom
"knows and understands all things, and will guide me

---

[16] Colledge and Walsh, trans., *Julian of Norwich Showings*, 229-230.
Julian of Norwich (1343-1416; dates uncertain) was an English mystic
and anchoress.

[17] Interestingly enough, the words "savor" and "wisdom" have the same
root; they come from the Latin word *sapere*, meaning "to taste or to
be wise."

discreetly in my affairs and safeguard me by her glory" (Wis 9:11).

Reflecting on the following questions may help you evaluate your experience of reflection and wisdom:

◊ What words, pictures, and/or images come to mind when you sit with the word "reflection"? With "wisdom"?

◊ When have you reflected on an experience in your life and been able to either see it in a different light or see another aspect of it that wasn't obvious initially? What was it like to see that experience either change or broaden?

◊ Reflect on (immerse yourself or reenter) a recent experience of liturgy that really struck you: some word, prayer, gesture, action, or object. What does that reflection do to your experience?

◊ What might keep you and your community from becoming more reflective? What might encourage you and your community to engage in more frequent reflection?

The embodiment of the components in this section is a life-time process. It does not happen all at once. However, becoming aware of each of them will enrich our work and inform our approach to all ministry. We must keep in mind that the fruit and virtues arise through God's initiative and ongoing action in our lives and work; they are not of our own accord; they are a gift. These components and their accompanying fruits and virtues provide us with a strong foundation whether we are pastoral counselors or spiritual directors, pastoral or liturgical ministers.

Applying Pastoral Care
to Liturgical Renewal

How do these components and their fruits and virtues work in the area of liturgical renewal? In our renewal efforts, we assume many roles. We serve as models of prayer, reflection and sharing; we serve as teachers of content, doctrine and tradition; we serve as leaders of eucharistic liturgy itself and other forms of communal worship. Here is a brief but specific look at how the components of pastoral care can enhance our roles.

Models

We serve as models when our renewal efforts are directed toward helping people reflect on their experience of liturgy, share those reflections, and enter prayer more deeply.[18] Because many with whom we work are unfamiliar or uncomfortable with reflection, sharing and communal prayer, good modeling on our part is necessary. Our willingness to reflect on and share our own experience of liturgy will undergird this phase of our renewal efforts.

Regis Duffy says it well when he urges that,

> those who preach and teach must be willing to
> submit to the same questions they pose to
> others...willing to be disturbed from their
> complacency by the radical demands of the
> Gospel.[19]

What components of pastoral care will help us model most effectively?

---

[18] The importance of these three basic actions is discussed in Chapter 8.

[19] Duffy, *Real Presence*, 191.

A sense of *mutuality* is certainly necessary: we do not model from above but among. As we give, so do we receive. Mutuality encourages gratefulness for all those with whom we work. We see them as contributing to the process in different but equally significant ways. Thus mutuality brings the gift of humility to our work.

The component of *inclusiveness* is also necessary. When we model reflection, sharing and prayer, we are in a place where we can make everyone feel equally welcome and accepted. This inclusiveness fosters and is fostered by the gift of reconciliation. Modeling in a way that is mutual and inclusive creates and nurtures an atmosphere of freedom. When the people with whom we work begin to reflect, share and pray, they will do so more openly and with greater ease.

If we incorporate a willingness to accept *support and challenge* from others when we model reflection, sharing and prayer, we encourage those whom we serve to do the same. Their willingness to accept support and challenge will liberate them from complacency and status quo.

Teachers

We serve as teachers of content when our renewal efforts are directed toward instruction, purpose and doctrine. Two components of pastoral care are critical when we teach:

◊ our faithfulness to God's call to be not just a community but a *covenant community*, a community bound together by God's promise

◊ our belief in the *prophetic vision* of ourselves as the embodiment of Christ, the Body of Christ

We must bring these components into our teaching of liturgy. In our teaching, we need to communicate how liturgy forms, informs and strengthens this covenant community (Body of Christ) and in turn how the community forms, informs and strengthens liturgy. They are inseparable. We must speak to the Christ within each person we teach. Before all else, we need to communicate that we are always taking part in the holy process of becoming Body of Christ.

Leaders

When renewal is directed toward prayer, we function as leaders of that prayer, of the community we serve. In leading, we must make every effort to incorporate the component of *inclusiveness*—all must be brought to the table lovingly. This component of pastoral care is perhaps the most important when we lead; no one must be forgotten. Further, as was stated before, inclusiveness brings to us the gift of reconciliation.

As leaders, we are the instruments who guide our assemblies, who prepare an environment in which real communal prayer, relationship with God, will thrive. The component of *reflection* is also essential to balanced, effective leadership. It is often in our own quiet reflections, in our savoring, in our willingness to simply be in the experience of worship that this intimate relationship with God is revealed and wisdom is born. This "wisdom made perfect" becomes the silent, steady hand in our leadership. When we pray with others, this gift of wisdom will be our guide as we guide.

From the outset, a certain attitude and approach will shape our renewal efforts, whether we are involved with prayer, reflection, or sharing; programs or projects; liturgical praxis, gestures, symbols, music, environment or catechesis. If our approach and attitude is one of *orientation toward growth*—an orientation that all humans possess by their very nature—the process will be greatly enhanced and facilitated. An orientation toward growth, a way of seeing every effort as an effort that arises from an unspoken desire to come to rest in God, points us into the light of the risen Christ.

It is a forward-looking orientation rather than an orientation arising out of sin, darkness and a need to fix. The difference is subtle but significant. Every renewal effort begs to arise from the desire to support human beings in their journey toward becoming one with the God who so loves them. Arising from this desire, our renewal will be about wholeness and holiness, about passion and life, about involvement and commitment to be all that God created us to be.

APPENDIX A

Developmental Theory Chart

There are many charts that depict the various developmental theories. I have used the basic structure of those found in Walter Conn's *Christian Conversion* (page 37) and James Fowler's *Stages of Faith* (page 52).

ERIKSON *Psychosocial Development* Functional/ Epigenetic	PIAGET *Cognitive Development* Structural/ Hierarchical	KOHLBERG *Moral Development* Structural/ Hierarchical
(1) TRUST/MISTRUST "Hope"	SENSORIMOTOR	AMORAL
(2) AUTONOMY/SHAME & DOUBT "Will"		
(3) INITIATIVE/GUILT "Purpose"	PREOPERATIONAL/ INTUITIVE	(1) PUNISHMENT/ OBEDIENCE
Emergence of the inner voice of guidance, the superego, which is often more punishing than external authorities; sibling rivalry; new patterns of sex-role socialization.	Differentiation of self from others; language development makes it possible to explore experiences, express feelings; person is unable to co-ordinate more than one point of view and is thus egocentric. Side by side play, non-interactive; ability to distinguish fact from fantasy somewhat limited.	Decides right and wrong based on punishment or reward to self. No ability to evaluate actions as they affect others because individual is egocentric. "Criteria such as physical size and visible symbols of authority are employed to determine who should be listened to."[1]
		PRECONVENTIONAL: (2) INSTRUMENTAL/ RELATIVIST
(4) INDUSTRY/ INFERIORITY "Competence" "Fundamentals of technology are developed, as the person becomes ready to handle the utensils, etc. used by the big people."[4] Systematic instruction/education. Mastery of these basic skills leads to competence.	CONCRETE OPERATIONAL Emergence of logical operations, which is the ability to do something and reverse it, generalize about it; thinking focuses on what is; there is an awareness of other that begins to take into account his/her perspective.	System of mutuality; "recognition that in order to get others to assent to or even to cooperate in the achievement of one's goals, one must be prepared to reciprocate."[5] Person more focused on other than before.

FOWLER *Faith* *Development* Structural/ Hierarchical	KEGAN *Ego* *Development* Structural/ Hierarchical	CONN *Conversions*
UNDIFFERENTIATED	INCORPORATIVE "I am my reflexes."	

(1) INTUITIVE/ PROJECTIVE "The Innocent"[2]
The only way of knowing is through concrete symbol and image; thought process is fluid; use of imagination to begin to make sense of the world; dawning self-awareness; "powerfully influenced by stories of faith of primally related adults."[3]

(1) IMPULSIVE "I have reflexes." "I am my impulses."
The person is its impulses— there is no distinction; tantrums possess the child and not visa-versa; yearning to be over-included in the love of one parent.

(2) MYTHIC/ LITERAL "The Literalist"
Ability to distinguish between reality and make believe; "Symbols are taken as one-dimensional and literal"[6]; story is the way one makes sense of the world; "religious imagery is often very real"[7]; no ability to reflect.

(2) IMPERIAL "I have impulses." "I am my needs."
The person is its needs; manipulation of the other who is "an instrument by which I satisfy my needs and work my will."[8]

PREMORAL ORIENTATION
Radically egocentric; all decisions are based on what is valuable and helpful for me.

ERIKSON *Psychosocial* *Development* Functional/ Epigenetic	PIAGET *Cognitive* *Development* Structural/ Hierarchical	KOHLBERG *Moral* *Development* Structural/ Hierarchical
	EARLY FORMAL	**(3) INTERPERSONAL CONCORDANCE**
(5) IDENTITY/ CONFUSION "Fidelity" Need for strong affiliation with a group as a means of achieving identity; primary concern is what one "appears to be in the eyes of others as compared with what they feel they are"[17]; commitment to friends, future work roles, significant group.	"Thinking takes wings"[9]; movement beyond empirical experience; ability to construct ideal states & abstract; to reflect on personal experience from outside rather than within; this has been called "intellectual transcendence."[10]	Actions are labeled right and chosen if they please others who are significant; "Caring for others and the need to be a good person, in one's own eyes as well as other's, is important."[11]
	FULL FORMAL	***CONVENTIONAL:* (4) AUTHORITY/ SOCIAL ORDER**
	Continues the development and construction mode cited in early formal; the context of experience is relative, ambiguous, contradictory; the construct of ideal states will accommodate reality; ability to critically reflect is fully developed.	Movement beyond the interpersonal into societal realm; the social perspective is no longer that of the other but that of society; decisions are made based on that which is "defined by law or the rules governing roles."[18]
		(4½) RELATIVIST Law, customs, group experiences are relative—rules become relativized.
(6) INTIMACY/ ISOLATION "Love" Once an individual has achieved his/her identity, he/she is ready to share that identity in an intimate way, which is the "capacity to commit to concrete affiliations and partnerships and to develop the ethical strength to abide by such commitments, even though they may call for significant sacrifices and compromises."[21]	**CONTEXTUAL/ DIALECTIC**	***POSTCONVENTIONAL:* (5) SOCIAL CONTRACT** While recognizing the relativity of values that the 4½ sees, this stage is "oriented to overall principles of utility, committed to the 'greatest good for the greatest number.'"[22] The realization of the relativity coupled with the ability to be critically reflective allows for the possibility of change in the contract that would not be considered at lower stages.

FOWLER	KEGAN	CONN
Faith	*Ego*	*Conversions*
Development	*Development*	
Structural/	Structural/	
Hierarchical	Hierarchical	

(3) SYNTHETIC/ CONVENTIONAL "The Loyalist"	(3) INTERPERSONAL "I have needs." "I am my relationships."	(1) [UNCRITICAL] MORAL
"What is important is doing it with the group"[12]; belief system is uncritically adopted; conformist, "tuned to the expectations & judgments of others"[13]; authority comes from group.	Person finds completion in the groups to which she belongs; "if key relations end or central roles collapse or are lost, persons of this stage are put at serious risk."[14] "I am my relationships, I am my roles." "The other is necessary to bring the self into being. This is fusion, not intimacy."[15]	No longer is decision based on what is good for me, but on a value. The content will vary (the value adopted) but the emphasis is on the shift from me to other. Choice or conversion enables one to view oneself in light of that value; this often "discloses the gap between the self we are and the self we should be."[16]

(4) INDIVIDUATIVE/ REFLECTIVE "The Critic"	(4) INSTITUTIONAL "I have relationships." "I am my organization."	
Authority for self is internalized and belief system is questioned; loss of meaning and inability to relate to the transcendent through symbol; "critical reflection on identity and outlook."[19]	One claims oneself as author of one's own life. Emphasis on self ownership; self-dependence. "The primacy of control inhibits mutuality and is still far from intimacy."[20]	

	(5) INTERINDIVIDUAL "I have control." "I am myself."	(2) AFFECTIVE
	This is the fully mature individual; is separate and yet able to share; full intimacy is possible. This stage establishes a model for "authentic human autonomy and unconditional surrender."[23] There is "a commingling which guarantees distinct identities."[24]	With a self to give comes the ability to relocate the concentration on self to concern for others. Conn simply equates this conversion with falling in love; the conversion itself is very complex if it is authentic; it is reflective, it is a deliberate decision, not a chance happening; it will express itself in selfless, loving service.

ERIKSON *Psychosocial Development* Functional/ Epigenetic	PIAGET *Cognitive Development* Structural/ Hierarchical	KOHLBERG *Moral Development* Structural/ Hierarchical
(7) GENERATIVITY/ STAGNATION **"Care"** This stage includes productivity and creativity, but primarily focuses on the desire and ability to "guide and establish the next generation."[25] Accomplishment of this task means that a "narrowness of self-concern"[26] has been transcended.		**(6) UNIVERSAL ETHICAL PRINCIPLES** "Universal principles of justice, of the reciprocity and equality of human rights, and of respect for the dignity of human beings as individual persons."[27] Moral imagination that determines what is manifestly fair must be detached from self-interests.
(8) EGO INTEGRITY/ DESPAIR **"Wisdom"** Integrity "loves life in the face of death."[31] Beyond that is the sense that as each one's individual life is lived, so is all of life; a post-narcissistic love arises that is "part of a world order and grounded in spiritual depth."[32] "Healthy children will not fear life if their elders have integrity enough not to fear death."[33]		**(7) RELIGIOUS** This stage is a recent formulation; it attempts to answer the question, "Why be moral?" This moves beyond the humanistic model of life into a cosmic one; "we value life from its standpoint"[34] rather than our own.

FOWLER	KEGAN	CONN
Faith	*Ego*	*Conversions*
Development	*Development*	
Structural/	Structural/	
Hierarchical	Hierarchical	

(5) CONJUNCTIVE

"The Seer"
"Willingness to let reality speak its word,"[28] regardless of the impact it has on the knower; openness to that which is other; "symbolic power is reunited with conceptual meanings"[29]; an increasing sense of relativity; developing vision of that which has not yet been realized causes tension/ paradox.

(3) COGNITIVE [CRITICAL MORAL]

In uncritical moral conversion, the value assumed is determined by external authority. Here, what is valuable is determined by oneself; "In the moral life, one must be one's own tailor, regardless of the brilliance of one's favorite designer."[30]

(6) UNIVERSALIZING

"The Saint"
Radical commitment and vision that incorporates the transcendent, divine plan of universal love; willingness to sacrifice self for this plan; "the eschatological vision that characterizes people in Fowler's stage six of faith is for me the inspiration of all faith and sacrament."[35] "Total commitment to the ongoing, guiding presence of God or whatever the person recognizes as Ultimate Authority."[36]

(6) GOD-GROUNDED

"I relinquish myself."
Robert Kegan does not go beyond the Interindividual Self. However, Fowler describes this self as he sees it evolving in his Universalizing Stage. Self is no longer the center of being; Autonomy becomes relative to God & person is free to choose unity with God while maintaining a sense of self. There should be a "yearning that all creation should be complete & all God's creatures should be one."[37]

(4) [CHRISTIAN] RELIGIOUS

Here is the apex of conversion: (1) the moral conversion is the decision not to choose what is good for self but to choose that which has value; (2) affective is the radical focus on total loving service of the other; (3) cognitive locates the authority for the value within self; (4) religious involves the self, affectively converted, choosing its value and focus to be God; in losing oneself in God, one finds oneself.

ENDNOTES FOR
DEVELOPMENTAL THEORY CHART

1. Fowler, *Stages*, 58.
2. The names for Fowler's stages (in quotation marks) were developed in Charles McCullough's book, *Heads of Heaven, Feet of Clay*. I found them in Kenneth Stokes' book, *Faith Is a Verb*.
3. Fowler, *Stages*, 133.
4. Erikson, *Childhood and Society*, 261.
5. Fowler, *Stages*, 66.
6. Ibid., 149.
7. Stokes, *Faith Is a Verb*, 16.
8. Joann Wolski Conn, *Spirituality and Personal Maturity*, 55.
9. Walter Conn, *Christian Conversion*, 50.
10. Fowler, *Stages*, 71.
11. Walter Conn, *Christian Conversion*, 52.
12. Ibid., 58.
13. Fowler, *Stages*, 173.
14. Kegan, *The Evolving Self*, 100.
15. Ibid.
16. Walter Conn, *Christian Conversion*, 28.
17. Erikson, *Childhood and Society*, 262.
18. Fowler, *Stages*, 79.
19. Ibid., 183.
20. Joann Wolski Conn, *Spirituality and Personal Maturity*, 56.
21. Erikson, *Childhood and Society*, 262.

22. Fowler, *Stages*, 83.
23. Walter Conn, *Christian Conversion*, 225.
24. Kegan, *The Evolving Self*, 105.
25. Erikson, *Childhood and Society*, 266.
26. Walter Conn, *Christian Conversion*, 58.
27. Ibid., 61.
28. Fowler, *Stages*, 185.
29. Ibid., 197.
30. Walter Conn, *Christian Conversion*, 127.
31. Ibid., 58.
32. Fowler, *Stages*, 86.
33. Erikson, *Childhood and Society*, 269.
34. Walter Conn, *Christian Conversion*, 219.
35. Duffy, *Real Presence*, 71.
36. Stokes, *Faith Is a Verb*, 22.
37. Fowler, *Faith Development*, 76.

APPENDIX B

On Being "Church"

The following article[1] by Rosemary Radford Ruether addresses the feelings that many people seem to be struggling with today in regard to being Catholic. I find her insights to be sensitive and consoling, honest and heartfelt.

> How can I remain a Catholic given the evils of this church?
>
> I think it is helpful to sort out what...we are really asking in this question. Are we really asking how we are able to be in relation to God, to Christ?
>
> Surely, we know that God is as available to us sitting under a tree as sitting in a church building. Jesus said, "Wherever two or three are gathered in my name, I am there in the midst of you." We are the church and Christ is present with us wherever we gather in his name.
>
> So the real issue is not relation to God or Christ or even being the church. The issue is the *government* of the institutional church. It is this that has a

---

[1] Ruether, "What to do if church is an 'occasion of sin'?" *National Catholic Reporter* 28, no. 34 (July 17, 1992): 22.

non-participatory, patriarchal organization and is failing to provide positive ministry for many of us.

Once it is clear that the problem is the governments of the institutional (Roman Catholic) church, then we can refocus the core issues. How do we find nurturing ministry, the experience of gathering as the people of God and also the mandates to be a ministering people in a badly run institution?

There are several possible answers. One, we look around to find a local church which is doing a fairly good job of being sensitive to justice and love, and join it. Or we gather a few friends and create a community that we ourselves generate for prayer and discussion, or we operate with some combination of the two.

We need to be clear that being the church has nothing to do with accepting violence and oppression from ecclesiastical governments. This is the opposite of authentic ministry. It is the negation of the presence of Christ. When this is happening, Christ is not present or present incognito with the injured and suffering ones. We should not tolerate such antiministry, especially in the name of Christ and the church.

So I think we need to be clear about our priorities. In my view, our first priorities are to receive life-giving ministry and to give it to others. We need to take care of ourselves. This means avoiding places of antiministry where we leave feeling angry, hurt, frustrated and bitter. These, to use traditional Catholic language, are "occasions of sin."

This means finding communities of love and justice, communities that give us glimpses of our creative and redeemed life. We need then to connect ourselves with groups where we can mediate some of this redemptive life to others in service.

Then, when we have our own lives properly centered and in good relations to what we can do for others, we might take on, as part of our ministry, some work to alleviate the violence of ecclesiastical institutions and help to create some spaces in these institutions for doing a better job of ministry.

But we shouldn't get too obsessed or frustrated with this task. We should keep it in its place. Like a tithe, we should see it as worth about 10 percent of our energy, and then only at the point when we are healed enough ourselves to have a genuine "surplus."

●

BIBLIOGRAPHY

Baldovin, John, S.J. *Worship: City, Church, and Renewal.* Washington, D.C.: The Pastoral Press, 1991.

Barry, William A., S.J. *God and You: Prayer as Personal Relationship.* Mahwah, New Jersey: Paulist Press, 1987.

Barry, William A., S.J., and William J. Connolly, S.J. *The Practice of Spiritual Direction.* San Francisco: Harper and Row, 1982.

Becker, Ernest. *Denial of Death.* New York: Free Press, 1973.

Blakney, Raymond, trans. *Meister Eckhart.* New York: Harper Torchbooks, 1941.

Campbell, Joseph, with Bill Moyers. *The Power of Myth.* New York: Doubleday, 1988.

Carroll, L. Patrick, S.J., and Katherine M. Dyckman, S.N.J.M. *Inviting the Mystic, Supporting the Prophet.* Ramsey, New Jersey: Paulist Press, 1981.

Ciferni, Andrew D., O.Praem. *This Saving Cup.* Washington, D.C.: Federation of Diocesan Liturgical Commissions, 1991.

Clinebell, Howard. *Basic Types of Pastoral Care and Counseling: Resources for the Ministry of Healing and Growth.* Nashville, Tennessee: Abingdon Press, 1984.

Coles, Robert. *Dorothy Day: A Radical Devotion.* Reading, Massachusetts: Addison-Wesley, 1987.

Colledge, Edmund, O.S.A., and James Walsh, S.J., trans. *Julian of Norwich Showings.* The Classics of Western Spirituality Series. Ramsey, New Jersey: Paulist Press, 1978.

Collins, Mary, O.S.B. *Worship: Renewal to Practice.* Washington, D.C.: The Pastoral Press, 1987.

Conn, Joann Wolski. *Spirituality and Personal Maturity.* Mahwah, New Jersey: Paulist Press, 1989.

Conn, Walter. *Christian Conversion: A Developmental Interpretation of Autonomy and Surrender.* Mahwah, New Jersey: Paulist Press, 1986.

Cooke, Bernard. "Sacraments." *The New Dictionary of Sacramental Worship.* Ed. Peter Fink, S.J. Collegeville, Minnesota: Liturgical Press, 1991.

Driver, Tom. *The Magic of Ritual.* New York: HarperSan Francisco, 1991.

Duffy, Regis A. "Formative Experience and Intentional Liturgy." *Studies in Formative Spirituality* 3 (November 1982): 351-361.

_____. *Real Presence: Worship, Sacraments and Commitment.* New York: Harper and Row, 1982.

Edwards, Tilden. *Spiritual Friend: Reclaiming the Gift of Spiritual Direction.* Mahwah, New Jersey: Paulist Press, 1980.

Egan, Harvey, S.J. *Christian Mysticism: The Future of a Tradition.* New York: Pueblo Publishing Company, 1984.

Emminghaus, Johannes H. *The Eucharist: Essence, Form, Celebration.* Collegeville, Minnesota: Liturgical Press, 1976.

Empereur, James. *Worship: Exploring the Sacred.* Washington, D.C.: The Pastoral Press, 1987.

Erikson, Erik. *Childhood and Society.* New York: W. W. Norton & Co., 1963.

Fink, Peter, S.J. *Worship: Praying the Sacraments.* Washington, D.C.: The Pastoral Press, 1991.

_____. "Imagination and Worship." *The New Dictionary of Sacramental Worship.* Ed. Peter Fink, S.J. Collegeville, Minnesota: Liturgical Press, 1991.

Fowler, James W. *Faith Development and Pastoral Care.* Philadelphia: Fortress Press, 1987.

_____. *Stages of Faith: The Psychology of Human Development and the Quest for Meaning.* San Francisco: Harper and Row, 1981.

Gallen, John, S.J. "Assembly." *The New Dictionary of Sacramental Worship.* Ed. Peter Fink, S.J. Collegeville, Minnesota: Liturgical Press, 1991.

Greeley, Andrew M. "Good Liturgy Is Little More Than a Good Weave." *National Catholic Reporter* 26, no. 21 (March 16, 1990): 12-13.

Guzie, Tad. "Reclaiming the Eucharist." *Liturgy* 7, no. 1 (Summer 1987): 29-33.

Harrington, Daniel, S.J. "Baptism in Scripture." *The New Dictionary of Sacramental Worship.* Ed. Peter Fink, S.J. Collegeville, Minnesota: Liturgical Press, 1991.

Haughton, Rosemary. *The Passionate God.* New York: Paulist Press, 1981.

_____. *The Transformation of Man.* Springfield, Illinois: Templegate Publishers, 1980.

Hovda, Robert. *Dry Bones.* Washington, D.C.: The Liturgical Conference, 1973.

_____. *There Are Different Ministries.* Washington, D.C.: The Liturgical Conference, 1975.

Hughes, Kathleen, C.S.J. "Liturgy and Justice: Bridging the Gap." *Modern Liturgy* 18, no. 8: 9-11.

Irwin, Kevin. *Liturgy, Prayer and Spirituality.* New York: Paulist Press, 1984.

Johnson, Lawrence. *The Word and Eucharist Handbook.* San Jose, California: Resource Publications, Inc., 1986.

Kavanagh, Aidan. *On Liturgical Theology.* New York: Pueblo Publishing Co., 1984.

Kegan, Robert. *The Evolving Self—Problem and Process in Human Development.* Cambridge: Harvard University Press, 1982.

Kidd, Sue Monk. "The Story-Shaped Life." *Weavings* (Spring 1989): 19-26.

Lathrop, Gordon. "Chronicle: AIDS and the Cup." *Worship* 62, no. 2 (March 1988): 161-165.

_____. "How Symbols Speak." *Liturgy* 7, no. 1 (Summer 1987): 9-13.

Manly, Gregory, and Anneliese Reinhard. *The Art of Praying Liturgy.* Melbourne: Spectrum Publications, 1984.

McManus, Frederick. *Liturgical Participation: An Ongoing Assessment.* Washington, D.C.: Pastoral Press, 1988.

Merton, Thomas. *Seasons of Celebration.* New York: Farrar, Straus, and Giroux, 1965.

Michael, Chester P., and Marie C. Norrisey. *Prayer and Temperament.* Charlottesville, Virginia: The Open Door, Inc., 1984.

Moore, Sebastian. *Let This Mind Be in You: The Quest for Identity Through Oedipus to Christ.* New York: Harper and Row, 1985.

Ostdiek, Gilbert. *Catechesis for Liturgy.* Washington, D.C.: Pastoral Press, 1986.

_____. "Catechesis, Liturgical." *New Dictionary of Sacramental Worship.* Ed. Peter Fink, S.J. Collegeville, Minnesota: Liturgical Press, 1991.

Piil, Mary Alice. "Baptism, Ministers of." *The New Dictionary of Sacramental Worship.* Ed. Peter Fink, S.J. Collegeville, Minnesota: Liturgical Press, 1991.

Power, David N. "Liturgical Praxis: A New Consciousness at the Eye of Worship." *Worship* 4 (July 1987): 290-304.

Progoff, Ira. "Waking Dream, Living Myth." *Myths, Dreams and Religion.* Ed. Joseph Campbell. Dallas: Spring Publications, 1970.

Ramshaw, Elaine. *Ritual and Pastoral Care.* Philadelphia: Fortress Press, 1987.

Reuther, Rosemary Radford. "What to do if church is an 'occasion of sin'?" *National Catholic Reporter* 28, no. 34 (July 17, 1992): 22.

Schmemann, Alexander. *For the Life of the World.* Crestwood, New York: St. Vladimir's Seminary Press, 1973.

Schroth, R. A., S.J. "Media Mirrors Mixed Up America after Gulf War." *National Catholic Reporter* 28, no. 13 (January 31, 1992): 16.

Searle, Mark. "On the Art of Lifting up the Heart: Liturgical Prayer Today." *Studies in Formative Spirituality* 3 (November 1982): 399-410.

Simcoe, Mary Ann, ed. *The Liturgy Documents: A Parish Resource.* Chicago: Liturgy Training Publications, 1985.

Skublics, Ernest. "Psychologically Living Symbolism and Liturgy." *Carl Jung and Christian Spirituality.* Ed. Robert L. Moore. Mahwah: New Jersey: Paulist Press, 1988.

Stokes, Kenneth. *Faith Is a Verb: Dynamics of Adult Faith Development.* Mystic, Connecticut: Twenty-Third Publications, 1989.

Steindl-Rast, Brother David. *Gratefulness, the Heart of Prayer.* New York: Paulist Press, 1984.

Stone, Howard W. *The Word of God and Pastoral Care.* Nashville, Tennessee: Abingdon Press, 1988.

Thurian, Max. *The Mystery of the Eucharist.* Grand Rapids, Michigan: William B. Erdman's Publishing Co., 1984.

Turner, Victor. *The Ritual Process: Structure and Anti-Structure.* Baltimore: Penguin Books, 1969.

Webster's New Twentieth Century Dictionary of the English Language (Unabridged). 2nd ed. Ed. Jean L. McKechnie. N.p.: Collins World, 1977.

Williams, Margery. *The Velveteen Rabbit.* New York: Alfred A. Knopf, 1985.

INDEX

importance of intention in 43
personal 35-38
power of 45
promise of 46

Ruether, Rosemary Radford 73, 231

Sacraments
as formative 138
as revealing God's presence 47, 51-52, 143
as transformative 64, 138n, 143
post-Vatican Council II 51
pre-Vatican Council II 51

Sacred
action 52, 77
experience of 6, 75, 76, 124
relationship 53
space 53, 88

Sagan, Carl 168

Salvation
and developmental theory 145
bread as symbol of 110
story of 88

Schmemann, Alexander 72, 107

Scripture, praying with 68-69, 132-133, 189, 191-192

Self-awareness, and developmental theory 142, 148, 151, 152

Self-transcendence 144n, 211n

Service
as liturgy's call 195
to others 57-58

Sign of peace 95
as symbol 115

Sign of the Cross 95
as symbol 127

Silence
in worship 183, 188
purpose of 50

Skublics, Ernest 117

Spirituality, holistic 21

Stokes, Kenneth 145n

Story
and liberation 55-59, 60
Christian 56
promise of 56

Surrender, personal 38, 45-46, 61, 144n, 149, 152, 173

Symbolic
action 41, 123, 127, 129, 133
object 123
word 123, 126-127

Symbolic nature
of liturgy 7
of ritual 38, 39-41

Symbolic structure 23, 28
of Communion Rite 28

Symbolism
Christian, process of 127
heart of 23, 116
of cross 46
of Eucharist 20
of liturgy 23

Symbols
and experience 109-110, 124-125, 130
and imagination 185
and Jesus 130